C000186900

# Bubbe and Me in the Kitchen

this is what you want.
there is no onion soup mix
- carrot & celery. salt - pepper garlic.
der & over meat. Cover and
20 minutes per pound & med
Long + Kisses — M

hell

move

red

½ hr

# Bubbe AND Me
## *in the Kitchen*

A Kosher Cookbook of
Beloved Recipes and Modern Twists

MIRI ROTKOVITZ

Photography by Evi Abeler
Food styling by Laurie Knoop

SONOMA
PRESS

Copyright © 2016 by Miri Rotkovitz

No part of this publication may be reproduced, stored in a retrieval system, or transmitted in any form or by any means, electronic, mechanical, photocopying, recording, scanning, or otherwise, except as permitted under Sections 107 or 108 of the 1976 US Copyright Act, without the prior written permission of the Publisher. Requests to the Publisher for permission should be addressed to the Permissions Department, Sonoma Press, 918 Parker St, Suite A-12, Berkeley, CA 94710.

LIMIT OF LIABILITY/DISCLAIMER OF WARRANTY: The Publisher and the author make no representations or warranties with respect to the accuracy or completeness of the contents of this work and specifically disclaim all warranties, including without limitation warranties of fitness for a particular purpose. No warranty may be created or extended by sales or promotional materials. The advice and strategies contained herein may not be suitable for every situation. This work is sold with the understanding that the Publisher is not engaged in rendering medical, legal, or other professional advice or services. If professional assistance is required, the services of a competent professional person should be sought. Neither the Publisher nor the author shall be liable for damages arising herefrom. The fact that an individual, organization, or website is referred to in this work as a citation and/or potential source of further information does not mean that the author or the Publisher endorses the information the individual, organization, or website may provide or recommendations they/it may make. Further, readers should be aware that websites listed in this work may have changed or disappeared between when this work was written and when it is read.

For general information on our other products and services or to obtain technical support, please contact our Customer Care Department within the US at (866) 744-2665, or outside the US at (510) 253-0500.

Sonoma Press publishes its books in a variety of electronic and print formats. Some content that appears in print may not be available in electronic books, and vice versa.

TRADEMARKS: Sonoma Press and the Sonoma Press logo are trademarks or registered trademarks of Callisto Media, Inc., and/or its affiliates, in the United States and other countries, and may not be used without written permission. All other trademarks are the property of their respective owners. Sonoma Press is not associated with any product or vendor mentioned in this book.

Photography by Evi Abeler
Food styling by Laurie Knoop
Author photo (page 261) by Dan Wagner

ISBN: Print 978-1-943451-04-3 | eBook 978-1-943451-05-0

Dedicated to the memories of Savta,
Bubbe, and Minnie Bubbe, who nourished
the family with love

*For Riva and Gabriel*

# CONTENTS

# INTRODUCTION

I was floored when I learned, several years after her death, that my grandmother was a short woman. Maybe it was her regal bearing, or her tremendous personality. Maybe it was my child's perspective, with its perpetual upward gaze, which convinced me she possessed a stature that far surpassed her 5 foot, 2 inch frame. Maybe it's that memory is figurative as much as it is literal, and this is why Ruth Morrison Simon, my mother's mother and the only grandmother I knew, always loomed so large in mine.

Though I was blessed to have her in my life for just 10 years, they were incredibly formative ones. At the table in her kosher kitchen, she introduced me to new foods, shared wisdom about the ingredients she loved, and let me "help," even when mess-making was my forte. She imparted lessons about manners (licking the iced tea spoon did not constitute cleaning it), nutrition (fish was "brain food"), and cultural awareness (people around the world had their own distinctive food traditions).

She shared tales of her travels, and inspired my own fascination with international cuisine. Her cooking followed the rhythms of the seasons, and of the Jewish calendar. Working on this book, I've come to realize just how deep and unceasing an influence she had.

What I didn't realize until the manuscript was nearly written was that this woman, who symbolized for me everything a Jewish grandmother should be, never knew her own bubbes. Her mother, Shifra, passed away shortly before my mother was born, so my mom and her sister were bubbe-less as well.

> *There's something universal about the way our grandmothers personalize our family stories while linking us to our greater heritages.*

When she became a grandmother herself, she had no direct family example to emulate.

And yet, she had her mother's recipes and, through them, a tether to generations of bubbes who came before her. She knew the flavor—literally—of how they'd nurtured her forebears, and shared it with us. The baby of her Russian Jewish family, my grandmother was the only sibling of seven to be born in the United States. She adored the traditional kosher Eastern European fare on which she was raised. But she was also fascinated with the foodways of Jews from around the globe. She upheld tradition, but looked forward; she was vested in America, and the modern state of Israel.

She'd have loved today's kosher landscape, and its atmosphere of (re)discovery. The embrace of seasonal, internationally-inspired fare has us challenging biases about what Jewish food is. Very old traditions feel fresh and exciting. But what's equally fascinating (and what some have pointed out for years) is that this spirit of creative experimentation has its roots in the very foundation of traditional Jewish cuisine. Throughout history, expulsions, dispersions, and widespread migrations have characterized the Jewish experience. Even as *kashrut* served as an anchor to Jewish practice wherever in the world we laid down roots, it also offered a framework for adapting and connecting to host cultures, while retaining our unique identity as a people.

There's no doubt that Jewish food is having a heyday. We're beginning to shift our gaze from surrounding cultures to each other. There's growing recognition that the labels Ashkenazi, Sephardi, and Mizrahi don't begin to describe the diversity of cuisines that make up the Jewish canon. Chefs at acclaimed (and generally non-kosher) restaurants are exploring traditional Jewish foods from throughout the diaspora. The press—and foodies—have trained their eyes on Yotam Ottolenghi, Michael Solomonov, Alon Shaya, and Einat Admony, with their exciting riffs on Israeli cuisine. Gorgeous cookbooks, nearly all with titles declaring their new or modern takes on kosher, are filling bookstore shelves, a testament to the literal and figurative hunger for a way of eating that has sustained the Jewish people for generation upon generation.

The truth is, a lot of us are looking to our grandmothers. Whether we called them Bubbe (as my great-grandmothers were known), Savta (the name my grandmother chose for herself), Grandma, Nana, Nonna, Oma, or something else, whether we knew them or wish we had, whether they were gourmet cooks or didn't have much interest in the kitchen, there's something universal about the way they personalize our family stories while linking us to our greater heritages. In these pages, several wonderful Jewish culinary professionals enthusiastically shared stories and recipes from their own grandmothers, and in doing so, sparked long-forgotten memories of my own. I hope that my family's stories, too, will do the same for you.

My grandmother's recipes, and the new ones they've inspired, are a thread between past and future, and a part of the tapestry we continue to weave as a family. I hope they'll serve you well as you gather to nurture and entertain family and friends. If, like my Savta, you find a few recipes you enjoy enough to make your own, scribbling adjustments in the margins as she did, so much the better.

# CHAPTER ONE

# My Family, Our People, a World of Recipes

I grew up in a kosher home. And for as long as I've had my own kitchens, I've made them kosher ones. Call it reflex, or comfort zone, or belief-driven practice—you'd be right on any and all counts. For me, kosher is a way to look back, and a way to look forward. It's a mooring in a morass of conflicting, confusing food advice. It's a structure, a framework for channeling culinary indecision or inspiration. And it's a connection to Jews around the world and throughout time.

I think I was in high school the first time I heard someone quip about the "gastronomic Jew." It's a striking term I've heard countless times since. But whether used as a slight or owned as a badge of honor, the subtext was that otherwise non-observant Jews who professed a nostalgic fondness for kugel or lox (it was always Ashkenazi fare) couldn't possibly claim a meaningful connection to Judaism. That sentiment bothers me. Food is a means to connection and understanding—to other people, cultures, ideas and philosophies, and, yes, religion.

Food is a powerful conduit. Like my grandmothers before me, I understand cooking as a way to nurture, celebrate, heal, and gather family and friends together. My kids—ages two and seven, are young, but seem to understand that what our family eats is tied to our identity and traditions. Keeping kosher offers a touchpoint for their curiosity and questions about who we are and what's important to us. I hope it will also help them find their own sense of meaning as they figure out who they are.

## THOSE WHO CAME BEFORE

I was named for my father's mother, Doris—yes, etymological gymnastics were involved—who died before I was born. Doris was too busy selling fine housewares to cook. But she didn't need to. While she concerned herself with the china and crystal trappings of a well-laid table, the bubbes who preceded her (her mother and mother-in-law) claimed the kitchen as their domain. My two great-grandmothers, known as Minnie Bubbe and Bubbe, were, I'm told, wonderful old-world cooks.

By the time I was born, Minnie Bubbe was gone and Bubbe was bedridden. I heard only occasional stories about their cooking—like the time my father's "pet" chicken disappeared from the yard. Minnie Bubbe claimed the dog was responsible, though it was she, and not Baron, who suffered from a prodigious bout of indigestion that night. And while my grandfather's pharmacist status allowed him, legally, to fill alcohol prescriptions during Prohibition, Bubbe ran afoul of the authorities after Prohibition's repeal for selling pre-dyed margarine at the family's bar.

Less dramatic, yet more important, were the dishes they prepared to nurture the family. As I started researching this book, relatives recalled Minnie Bubbe's spiced knaidlach, and Bubbe's gefilte fish, brisket, and chopped liver enriched with gribenes (chicken skin cracklings) slathered on homemade challah. For years, my father has nostalgically yearned for Bubbe's pickled eggplant, but no one knows how she made it. The bubbes' minds were their recipe repositories. They cooked with their senses. They did not record their techniques.

# KOSHER RULES, IN A NUTSHELL

The basic tenets of kashrut include the following:

1. All fruits, vegetables, whole grains, beans, legumes, and nuts (in their raw, unprocessed states) are kosher. Virtually all bugs are non-kosher, so in some Orthodox circles, certain fruits and vegetables have fallen out of favor due to concerns over potential infestation.

2. Only the meat of mammals with split hooves that chew their cud (for example cows, sheep, goats, bison, and deer) may be eaten. Milk from kosher animals is kosher.

3. Birds of prey are not kosher. Kosher birds include chicken, geese, ducks, and turkeys. Eggs from kosher birds are kosher, but generally need to be checked to ensure they do not contain blood.

4. Shechita—ritual slaughter—must be properly performed, and the meat or poultry must be kashered to draw out the blood. Blood of any kind is not kosher.

5. Only fish with both fins and removable scales are kosher. They do not require shechita.

6. Meat and dairy may not be cooked together or eaten at the same meal.

7. Produce, grains, beans and legumes, nuts, eggs, and fish are pareve, or neutral foods, and may be eaten with either meat or dairy. (Note that according to some, meat and fish may not be cooked or consumed together.)

## TOGETHER IN THE KITCHEN

My grandmother Ruth, the inspiration for my own cooking in general and this book in particular, was the only grandmother I knew. She was a different sort of eater, and a different sort of cook.

The baby of her own family, she was younger than the bubbes on my father's side. Like them, she maintained a kosher home and cooked many Eastern European Ashkenazi specialties. She was also a world traveler, fascinated by the foods of other lands, and by Jewish cuisine from around the world. As mother to two daughters, she transmitted her recipes to them, and later to me.

In the first 10 years of my life, I spent countless hours in her kitchen and at her table, helping her cook, tasting her food, and learning about the ingredients and recipes that excited her most, often vis-à-vis lessons about Jewish tradition.

## THE RECIPE BOX

I wandered into the food world accidently, by way of theater. A stint with a touring production drove home the importance of healthy eating for performers; seeking a day job more fulfilling than office temping, I decided to pursue a nutrition degree. But as my professional focus shifted from the scientific to the culinary, and my interests veered toward food history and culture, I got increasingly curious about my grandmother's recipes.

My aunt was guardian of the recipe box; I had to convince her I was trustworthy enough to take temporary possession of the collection. I was living in New York at the time, and despite promises that the collection would be safe in my hands, neither my aunt nor my mother would allow the recipes to leave Baltimore.

So it was only on a visit home, as I sat alone at my parents' dining room table, that I finally had the chance to look through an unassuming, slightly dented, hunter green index card box. Here was a time capsule, a fantastic primary source, a chance to reconnect with my beloved grandmother who'd passed away years before. I opened the box, sure I'd find her outrageous, long-lost rum cake recipe. It wasn't there. But I was surprised to discover a random collection of clippings—everything from brochures from the 1950s outlining what to do in case of nuclear disaster to recipes she'd probably never made.

# THE JEWISH CAKE THAT WASN'T
## ... OR WAS IT?

There are recipes so legendary within one's own family that it's hard to believe anyone else makes them. Savta's apple cake (see page 212) is one of those. A holiday must-have, it conjures memories of her saucy raised eyebrow and easy smile. Her recipe collection included several copies written in her hand, in various states of readability. She probably had it memorized, yet whenever an oil drip or batter splotch rendered it impossible to read, she copied it over. I took this as a clue to the recipe's importance, and assumed it had been passed down through the family for generations.

It turns out the cake is not unique to my family—and its history is murky. I used to wonder how a cake could be "Jewish"—vesting an inanimate baked good with religion just seemed silly—but the descriptor may be a clue to its provenance. Many food historians believe the cake's origins are really Polish or Pennsylvania Dutch. The estimable food writer Joan Nathan tracked down the recipe in church cookbooks from two tiny Maryland towns. Some suppose the cake was dubbed "Jewish" because it eschewed the use of butter (or lard) and milk, in favor of oil and orange juice—ingredients that made the recipe attractive to kosher cooks, who could serve it after meals with meat.

Of course, that begs the question of who got the recipe from whom. Was it "Jewish" because kosher cooks adopted it, or because someone's bubbe passed it along to a non-Jewish friend?

In an article for *The Forward*, Nathan wrote that while researching her book *Quiches, Kugels, and Couscous*, she discovered yet another Jewish apple cake, made by a Jewish Parisian from her Polish mother's recipe. It proved strikingly similar to a cake made by non-Jewish Polish people. I suspect the cake is a classic example of culinary dialogue between Jews and their non-Jewish neighbors, and proof that a great recipe has universal appeal.

I realized I couldn't assign equal significance to everything that caught her eye, but I *was* getting a glimpse of the sorts of things that piqued her interest. At some point, the recipes went back to my aunt. The box was discarded, along with the random clippings. I asked about the recipes over the years, but it was only for the sake of this book that I was entrusted with the originals again. As I recall how I pored over slips of paper and index cards written in my grandmother's familiar hand, I'm grateful that I once got the chance to see all of the other things she'd tucked away among her treasured recipes—and especially that we still have the recipes, the most important things from that box.

Very recently, I learned that although Bubbe, my paternal great-grandmother, never wrote down her recipes, some had likely been preserved too. Her daughter, my Aunt Esther, didn't keep kosher, but recorded several family recipes, many of them kosher for Passover. Interestingly, a large proportion of my grandmother's special recipes were for Passover use, too. For women who learned to cook confidently sans cookbooks, Pesach—with its additional kosher strictures and unusual ingredients—was probably the one time of year they really appreciated the help of written recipes.

## "HEALTHY" KOSHER EVOLVES

There was a cookbook in my mom's collection I loved poring over. Unlike most cookbooks published in the 1970s and '80s, every page featured large, full-color photos of delicacies from around the globe. I was transfixed by recipes for the Turkish eggplant dish *imam bayildi*, Welsh rarebit, and a very elaborate French gateau. Having tackled the simple rarebit, I was itching to try my hand at layers of genoise, chocolate mousse, whipped cream, ganache, and chocolate shavings.

I got my mom's permission to make the cake for a dinner party, though my parents were dubious about my chances for success. We needed a pareve (milk-free) dessert to cap off a meat meal, and the recipe was practically an ode to dairy ingredients. I was probably about 9 or 10 at the time, but I was confident and forged ahead, baking the cake with margarine, Rich Whip, non-dairy creamer, and pareve dark chocolate (perhaps the only quality ingredient in the whole affair). This was back when eating "healthy" meant shunning ostensibly artery-clogging butter in favor of margarine. Yet the highly processed nature of the ingredients I used wasn't lost on me. I dubbed the concoction "Chemical Cake," and was pretty tickled that it fooled everyone who tasted it.

Culinary sleights of hand like this were pretty common on the kosher scene when I was growing up. Shabbat and holiday meals nearly always featured meat, yet desserts *looked* dairy-based. We dolloped faux whipped cream on margarine-based cakes, and swooned over Tofutti. As vegetarian analogs for cheese, pepperoni, and ground beef hit the market, some enjoyed the titillating thrill of eating "fake treif" like "cheese" burgers (with a Tofutti milk shake , natch), or "pepperoni" pizza.

Products like these gained traction, too, thanks to their theoretically healthier nutrition profile. Motivated by the belief that animal fat was inherently dangerous, many grandmothers abandoned schmaltz for Nyafat (a vegetarian substitute, but a veritable trans fat bomb), butter for margarine, eggs for Egg Beaters.

## *Kosher Today*

Old-world recipes, however well loved, were rarely touted as healthy. Yet the from-scratch (and often nose-to-tail) cooking in which our grandmothers and great-grandmothers were so well-versed was more in line with today's emphasis on whole foods and healthy living than they might have imagined. When I was in graduate school studying nutrition, scientists turned a critical eye on trans fats, and new studies illuminated the role of diet in inflammation. The Maimonidean exhortation to "Let nothing which can be treated by diet be treated by other means" felt especially timely.

With today's renaissance in farmers' markets, emphasis on heirloom and local produce, interest in pastured meats, and vogue for artisanal, small batch foodstuffs, we seem to be coming full circle in terms of the foods our forebears would have recognized and loved. Fortunately, the trend toward using whole foods is one that's a boon for our health. And it's one that offers fabulous opportunities for the kosher cook.

The truth is that while modern food processing raises lots of complicated kosher questions, a kosher lifestyle *can* be an exercise in simplification. Like my fellow nutritionists, I recommend shopping the perimeter of the supermarket—where "real" food lives—and using a sharp eye if you foray into the middle aisles, which are filled with processed products. Ingredients matter more than the supposed nutrition claims emblazoned on a package.

The same principle works with kashrut: Many single-ingredient foodstuffs in their raw or minimally processed state are kosher, whether or not they bear certification. (Of course, talk to your rabbi if you've got questions about what's considered acceptable in your community.) If you want to play with pareve "milk" and "meat" analogs, skip the ones built on high-fructose corn syrup, isolated soy protein, and MSG. Thanks to the growing interest in vegetarian and vegan diets, better options made of nuts, tofu, and grains abound. Build meals around produce, whole grains, legumes, and nuts, and you'll save time hunting for kosher products—and eat healthier, too.

# WHO'S BUYING KOSHER?

Food processing has become incredibly complex. Globalized ingredient sourcing, industrialized manufacturing processes, and convoluted labeling laws have conspired to complicate the question of whether a product is kosher. This has paved the way for a robust, highly sophisticated kosher certification industry. Interestingly, while that's a boon for those who keep kosher as a matter of religious conviction, observant Jews comprise only a tiny fraction of kosher consumers.

That the kosher certification industry has grown into a multibillion-dollar one is directly related to the fact that a tremendous number of consumers seek out kosher products, for many reasons.

1. Sometimes religion is a factor. Many observant Muslims buy kosher food, thanks to the overlap between halal and kosher rules (while halal certifications are gaining ground, kosher is more widespread in many countries). And some Christians commit to the basic biblical strictures of kosher law.

2. For vegetarians, vegans, and those with certain food allergies, kosher labeling can clarify whether a product is free of problematic ingredients.

3. Meat eaters may choose kosher products out of concern for animal welfare, as Jewish law takes a strong position against causing suffering to animals and requires swift, humane slaughter. (Those savvy to the realities of animal husbandry in today's world may also look beyond the neighborhood kosher butcher to a purveyor like Kol Foods or Grow and Behold for ethically raised and slaughtered kosher meat.)

4. There's also a widespread belief that the additional level of processing supervision translates to cleaner, safer food, though strictly speaking, this is not always the case.

# IN THE PANTRY

From my grandmother I learned the magic of a well-stocked pantry. Even if the fridge is practically empty (not that hers ever was), you can throw together a respectable meal with these basics. Note that once opened, some of these ingredients will take up residence in the refrigerator.

**BEANS AND LENTILS**  Stock up on both dried and canned beans—the former for slow cooking, the latter for convenience. Lentils cook quickly and don't need soaking, so I stick to dried. Do use caution if you use an electric slow cooker for dried beans, and kidney beans in particular. Slow cookers maintain temperatures that can significantly increase the toxicity of an illness-inducing antinutrient in dried beans called phytohemagglutinin. To be on the safe side, cook dry beans on the stove top at a hard boil for 10 minutes before draining, rinsing, and adding to slow cooker recipes. And don't eat raw or undercooked dry beans.

**BROTH OR STOCK**  Keep vegetable broth and/or chicken stock on hand (even if you make your own chicken soup) for cooking. I prefer the kind sold in boxes, because once you open the box, it stores easily in the refrigerator.

**CANNED FISH**  Sardines and anchovies are small but mighty. Sardines are a great source of protein and omega-3s for salads and sandwiches. Anchovies practically melt into sauces and dressings, and deliver a serious dose of savory. Salmon and tuna are good to have on hand too.

**CONDIMENTS**  My grandmother was a total progressive on the condiment front. Like her, I treasure-hunt for condiments from around the world and when I find intriguing kosher options, I snatch them up. Dijon mustard, tamari soy sauce, tahini, and sriracha are among my go-to condiments. It's also very helpful to have ketchup, mayonnaise, wasabi, and hot sauce on hand.

**FLOUR**  Start with all-purpose and white whole-wheat. Depending on what you typically bake, bread flour, pastry flour, and rye flour are nice additions.

**GRAINS**  Thanks to surging nutritional and culinary interest in whole and heritage grains, options have gotten a lot more interesting since my grandmother's day. Stock a long-grained rice, such as basmati, and a short-grained one, like Arborio, black, or sushi rice. To make the recipes in this book, you'll also need farro, barley, quinoa, and oats. Polenta is another great (and gluten-free) option to have on hand.

**HERBS AND SPICES** Herbs and spices have the power not just to wake up our senses, but to completely transform a dish. Keep both fresh and dried herbs and spices on hand, as they have different flavor profiles. Fresh and dried garlic and ginger are must-haves. Stock your spice cabinet with dried basil, tarragon, thyme, marjoram, oregano, rosemary, cinnamon, nutmeg, poppy seeds, cumin, and smoked paprika. Herb and spice blends take a lot of the guesswork out of seasoning. Some of my favorites include curry powder, garam masala—an essential blend in Indian cuisine, Chinese five-spice powder, the seafood seasoning Old Bay, the Moroccan ras el hanout—which translates to "top of the shop," or the best spices a seller has to offer, and the Middle Eastern za'atar—which typically features sumac, thyme, oregano, and sesame seeds. Fresh herbs like basil, dill, parsley, chives, and cilantro are indispensable. Plunk store-bought bunches in a glass of water to keep them fresh for a few days, or better yet, grow your own for a steady supply.

**NUTS AND NUT BUTTERS, DRIED FRUIT, JAMS AND PRESERVES** For both sweet and savory recipes, I love to have a variety of nuts, natural nut butters, dried fruits, and preserves on hand. Almond, cashew, peanut, and sunflower butters are all great. Marmalade is another must-have. To preserve freshness, store nuts in the freezer, and transfer open nut butter and preserves to the fridge.

**OILS** You'll need extra-virgin olive oil and a neutral-flavored oil such as grapeseed, sunflower, avocado, or canola. Specialty oils such as coconut, toasted sesame, walnut, or hazelnut have their own rich and distinctive flavors, and make great additions to salad dressings, or for finishing dishes.

**PASTA** My pantry is stocked with Italian semolina pasta in an array of shapes, plus wide egg noodles for kugel, Israeli (pearl) couscous, and Asian noodle varieties like rice noodles and Japanese buckwheat soba.

**SALT AND PEPPER** Though my grandmother worried over salt, and many Americans eat far too much of it in processed food, it is still a valuable component of cooking. I prefer to use kosher salt or sea salt, which are a little lower in sodium than table salt. If you use table salt, use only half of what the recipes in this book recommend. For baking or recipes where I want the salt to mix uniformly into a dish, I like fine pink Himalayan sea salt, which is purer and richer in minerals than many other salts. For braising, roasting, soups, or finishing dishes, I like the flaked texture of kosher salt brands like David's or Diamond Crystal, or sea salts like Maldon. When it comes to pepper, buy whole peppercorns, and grind them as needed. Some jars have built-in grinders.

**SPECIALTY ITEMS** I love the way intriguing specialty ingredients inspire experimentation with new cuisines and delicious takes on old favorites. The recipes in this book call for nori (dried sheets of toasted seaweed), pickled ginger, rice paper wrappers, and pomegranate molasses. I also like to keep matcha tea, coconut milk, and plenty of chocolate on hand.

**SWEETENERS** You'll need sugar (I prefer evaporated cane sugar to white for its more dimensional flavor), brown sugar, confectioner's sugar, honey, pure maple syrup (dark grades), and date syrup (silan)—a very ancient sweetener.

**VEGETABLES** In jars—pickles, olives, capers, roasted peppers, artichokes, and hearts of palm.

**VINEGARS** For the basics, stock up on balsamic, red wine, rice, and apple cider vinegar.

### The Passover Pantry

Everything changes for Passover. Whether you scrub your kitchen and pantry from top to bottom before the holiday, or just toss the chametz and take out the Passover dishes, there's a lot of shopping to do. For a list of specific food substitutions for Passover, see page 238.

**BAKING** Must-haves include matzo meal and cake meal, potato starch, and ground nuts.

**SPICES** If you can't find your favorite ground spices with Passover certification, keep in mind that whole spices purchased before the holiday don't need it (though if you don't eat *kitniyot*—a category that also includes rice and legumes—during Passover, there are some you'll want to avoid).

**OTHER ESSENTIALS** Matzo, canned fish, jam, nut butters, nuts and dried fruit, oil, vinegar, and chocolate.

## SUPPORTING EQUIPMENT

The kosher prohibition against mixing milk and meat extends beyond the plate. Cookware, utensils, gadgets, serveware, and even sponges have to be separate too. So kosher cooks need more equipment (and storage space!) than average. But with strategic planning, you can outfit a kosher kitchen without buying out the housewares store.

Beyond the usual stockpots, saucepans, and skillets, here are some essentials. Give some thought to what you will use these items for, and you may be able to get away with one instead of two. (For example, you may need only one stand mixer or beater, if nearly all of your heavy-duty baking is dairy or pareve.)

**CAST IRON SKILLET(S)** These are the pans your great-grandmother used. Well-seasoned cast iron is naturally nonstick and has marvelous, even heat retention. It goes from the stove top to the oven with ease. From omelet making and pan roasting to latke frying, it's a workhorse that will get constant use.

**CHEF'S PAN(S) OR SAUCIERS** These large, wide, deep skillets are incredibly versatile. Use them for sautés and stir-frys, rice and risotto, steaming vegetables, and more.

**DUTCH OVEN** When it comes to cooking meat, a Dutch oven is wonderful for slow braises, stews, roasts like brisket, and even small batches of soup. (An electric slow cooker is another possibility, although a less versatile one.)

**IMMERSION BLENDER** Some swear by food processors, but between my chef's knife and an old-fashioned box grater, I rarely bother pulling mine out of the cabinet. An immersion (or stick) blender is a different animal, and can be very useful for tasks like puréeing soups right in the pot, and emulsifying sauces and dressings. Splurge on one with whisk and mini food processor attachments, and you can use it to whip egg whites or cream, and prep small batches of pesto, hummus, or ground nuts.

**KNIVES** My grandmother, and now my mom, somehow managed to cook with flimsy serrated paring knives. I didn't inherit that gene. A quality *paring knife* is essential for peeling and slicing fruits and vegetables and smaller scale, decorative prep work. A *serrated bread knife* is helpful too.

If there's one piece of kitchen equipment I can't do without, it's my *chef's knife*, a long knife with a wide, tapered blade. A sharp, high-quality 8- to 10-inch chef's knife is kitchen gold, useful for all sorts of prep work. If the knife has a riveted handle, look for a full tang, which means the metal from the blade runs through the end of the handle. (Note that there are some excellent knives, such as the Japanese Globals, that don't have a tang at all.) What's most important is that the knife is well balanced and feels good in your hand.

Unless you're vegetarian, you'll need separate meat and dairy knives, so consider buying different brands, or at least knives with different handles; the distinctive looks will help prevent mix-ups. Once you've invested in those, expand your collection with others as the need arises—for example, a boning knife to break down chicken or a fillet knife for skinning and boning fish.

**PEPPER MILL**  A good pepper mill is a must-have for freshly ground black pepper. I'm a fan of a coarse grind.

**RIMMED BAKING SHEETS**  Large rimmed baking sheets are so versatile and take up very little space. Use them for everything from baking cookies to roasting vegetables.

**STAND MIXER OR ELECTRIC BEATERS**  A stand mixer is a splurge, but worthwhile for avid bakers or bread makers. Electric beaters are a comparative steal; use them for mixing batters, whipping egg whites or cream, or making frostings.

## HER RECIPE, MY RECIPE, NEW RECIPES

My grandmother's recipe box—and her food philosophies and fascinations—are my inspiration, and you'll find some of her favorite recipes in this collection, along with modern riffs on treasured family dishes. I've also created lots of recipes that capitalize on ingredients she loved but had little access to (such as fresh asparagus), and ones she'd never have imagined, like quinoa.

Our shared love of international cuisine and curiosity about the creative kosher adaptations that have shaped Jewish foods throughout the diaspora are reflected here too, in fresh, healthy recipes that work for both busy weeknights and special occasions. I've also tried to pay tribute to a few of the bubbes' recipes, using collective family memories as clues to help recreate lost favorites. Each recipe is labeled Dairy, Meat, or Pareve; those that can be adapted to suit different types of meals will feature multiple designations and ingredient substitution suggestions. A great number of the recipes in this book are kosher for Passover, or can be easily adapted for the holiday. Some recipes have been written specifically for the Seder or with Passover dietary restrictions in mind; these can be found at the end of a handful of chapters. At the end of the book, I've included an index of kosher for Passover and Passover-friendly recipes, as well as seasonally inspired menu suggestions for Shabbat and holidays.

Whether you're a new or seasoned cook, I hope these recipes will bring you joy in the kitchen and around the table. And I hope the stories spark fond memories of your own loved ones and inspire you to enjoy old traditions—and create lots of delicious new ones—with family and friends.

IN THE KITCHEN WITH
# ALEXANDRA ZOHN

*I always thought my grandmother's charoset was the universal charoset. It wasn't until I spent my first Passover away from home that I realized the delicious dark, aromatic, nutty, fruity paste she made was hers only, and the most delicious there ever was.*

*Learned in her own grandmother's kitchen, the recipe was brought to Mexico from Turkey. I have no idea how many generations of women in the family made it year after year to remember the mortar used during the Hebrews' slavery days in Egypt. But as soon as I discovered that charoset was very different in every family's tradition, I asked my grandmother Rita to teach me how to make hers, ours.*

*I'm sure that back home, my great-great grandmother Rosa ground the dates, nuts, raisins, and apples by hand (maybe she even picked them from her own yard), and that she used homemade orange marmalade. My grandmother made a switch to an electric blender and store-bought jam. When I prepare it, I have a list of choices: immersion blender, power blender, food processor. Sometimes, when the holiday is rushing in and I run out of time, I cheat and use pre-ground nuts, prepared applesauce, and date paste. It doesn't matter. It still always takes me back to my grandmother's and my family table when I take the first bite.*

*I had to move to a different country, away from home, to realize that my family's treasures were unique. We always ate delicious homemade food, but I assumed that was how people everywhere ate, until I was invited to different households in a different country. My grandmother's recipes have allowed me to take a quick trip back to her table any time I need comfort or want to celebrate. The dishes fill my senses and cure my nostalgia. I guess the same happened to my great-great-grandmother, who had to leave everything behind in Smyrna to move to Mexico. Perhaps her charoset took her back home as well.*

**ALEXANDRA ZOHN** is a certified holistic health coach, food writer, and the founder and executive pastry chef of Three Tablespoons, a baking company specializing in nutritious treats.

# Rosa's Charoset

PAREVE
*Makes about 2 ½ cups*
*Prep time: 15 minutes*

1 organic Gala apple, peeled,
    seeded, and cubed *or* ¾ cup
    unsweetened applesauce

6 pitted dates

½ cup raisins

Juice of 1 orange

2 to 3 tablespoons orange marmalade
    (or apricot preserves)

3 tablespoons matzo meal

1 ½ cups ground nuts

Process all the ingredients in a food processor or blender until puréed or the desired consistency is achieved.

Or simply throw it all in a large 1-gallon zipper-top freezer bag, making sure there's no air trapped in the bag. Zip it closed and mush it with your hands, a rolling pin, your feet, or anything you want, until it turns into a paste. Kids love helping out with this task!

NOTE: *I like pecans, but walnuts, hazelnuts, or a mix work well too. Hemp seeds might be a good substitution if you can't use nuts.*

Three-Cheese Quiche with Caramelized
Onions and Spinach (page 39)

CHAPTER TWO

# Breakfast and Brunch

Breakfast at breakfast time was always a simple affair in my family—maybe we'd have a little cereal, some yogurt, or bread and cheese. On cold days, there was oatmeal, or cinnamon-dusted farina with raisins, a melting pat of butter at its center. Make no mistake, we're all big on breakfast fare—we just happen to like it for brunch time entertaining, or, better yet, dinner. When I offered my daughter an egg for breakfast recently, she looked at me stunned and said, "But that's not breakfast food!" And every year at Yom Kippur, as we break the fast with the same menu of lox, bagels, and veggies that my grandmother served, someone always announces, "Now this is my favorite kind of meal."

# Feinkuchen Egg Sandwich with Avocado

SERVES 1 HUNGRY PERSON, OR 2 GOOD SHARERS | DAIRY

*I was surprised to discover that Bubbe's most nostalgia-inducing recipe was for this simple egg sandwich. My Aunt Merle remembers eating it on kaiser rolls, my dad on rye bread. After my parents got engaged, my mom would stop by on her walk to work for a foil-wrapped bagel feinkuchen to eat on the way. As for the name, it's likely Bubbe's Yiddishized take on the German "fine cake," or possibly "good cooking." When I couldn't find any other reference to an egg sandwich with that name, I wondered if it was her own little joke—a comment on the ultra-easy preparation. Apparently, though, Bubbe wasn't known for her sense of humor. The way the family devoured the butter-slathered sandwiches, she may have dubbed them "feinkuchen" with serious pride. Somewhere along the line, my dad added chives: "Probably," he said, "because your mother likes them." The avocado is my own addition. Hot sauce would be nice too.*

*Prep time: 5 minutes*
*Cook time: 5 minutes*

2 slices rye bread, or a split challah roll or bagel

Unsalted butter, softened

2 large eggs

½ teaspoon snipped fresh or freeze-dried chives

Pinch sea salt or kosher salt

1 teaspoon extra-virgin olive oil

¼ avocado, sliced

Hot sauce (optional)

### Tip

If you plan to make several sandwiches, lower the heat to 225°F, so you can keep them warm without overcooking.

Preheat the oven to 300°F. Spread the softened butter on the rye bread or inside of the challah or bagel. Or do as Bubbe did, and generously butter both sides! Place on a piece of foil large enough to wrap the finished sandwich.

In a small bowl, beat the eggs, chives, and salt.

In a heavy skillet, warm the olive oil and a little butter over medium-high heat. Pour in the beaten eggs, and cook undisturbed for 1 to 2 minutes, or until the edges are set. Run a spatula around the omelet, and fold in half, then quarters. Cook 1 minute more, or just until cooked through.

Carefully transfer the omelet to a bread slice. Top with avocado and a second slice of bread, wrap in foil, and place in the oven for a few minutes, or until warmed through.

# Breakfast Quinoa with Berries

*I sometimes wonder what my grandmothers would have thought of ingredients like quinoa. Would a rediscovered ancient grain have enticed them, or passed beneath their notice, irrelevant to their recipes? Would they find it strange that to see a novel food became ubiquitous so soon after its introduction to the market? Or would they embrace it, coaxing it into a familiar recipe, like this honey-sweetened, berry-studded porridge?*

*Prep time: 5 minutes*
*Cook time: 25 minutes*

2 cups milk or soy milk

1 cup white or tri-color quinoa, rinsed

3 tablespoons honey, plus extra for serving

½ teaspoon cinnamon

1 cup fresh or frozen blueberries, chopped strawberries, raspberries, or a mix, plus extra for serving

### Note

If you opt for frozen blueberries, look for wild rather than cultivated berries, as they tend to be more flavorful. Note, too, that if the blueberries are not labeled organic, Canadian wild blueberries are less likely to be treated with pesticides than American berries.

In a medium saucepan set over medium-high heat, warm the milk or soy milk. When tiny bubbles begin to break the surface, stir in the quinoa. Bring to a boil, reduce the heat to low, and simmer, covered, until at least half the milk is absorbed and any white quinoa grains are partially translucent, about 13 to 15 minutes. (Red or black quinoa will not appear translucent, but the white ring surrounding them will begin to be visible.)

Add the honey and cinnamon, and stir to combine. Simmer uncovered, stirring occasionally, until the milk is mostly absorbed, the quinoa is tender, and small, whitish rings are visible around the grains, about 5 to 8 minutes more.

Gently stir in the berries, and simmer just until they are warmed through, about 1 minute. Divide the quinoa between four bowls, and serve with extra honey and berries if desired.

**STORAGE:** *Leftover breakfast quinoa may be refrigerated, covered, for up to 2 days. Reheat before serving.*

# Hot-Smoked Salmon Bagels with Herbed Goat Cheese and Veggies

SERVES 4 | DAIRY

*I'm all for a classic lox, bagel, and cream cheese sandwich, but sometimes it's nice to change things up just enough to keep it interesting. Hot-smoked salmon—dubbed "kippered salmon" at the appetizing shops of yore—has a drier, more toothsome texture than silky lox or cold-smoked salmon, but it has a lot of appeal, especially combined with crisp veggies, smooth avocado, and the creamy tang of goat cheese.*

*Prep time: 10 minutes*

4 bagels, split, toasted if desired

4 to 5 ounces herbed goat cheese or Boursin cheese

8 ounces sliced hot-smoked salmon

1 medium cucumber, peeled if desired, sliced into rounds

1 avocado, pitted and sliced

1 large red bell pepper, cored, seeded, and cut into strips

Freshly ground black pepper

Spread the bagel halves with goat or Boursin cheese. Divide the smoked salmon evenly among 4 bagel halves.

Top the 4 halves with the cucumber, avocado, and red pepper. Finish with a sprinkling of black pepper.

Top each sandwich with a second bagel half and press down lightly. Serve immediately, or refrigerate, wrapped, for up to 6 hours.

> **Tip**
>
> Substitute lox or cold-smoked salmon, such as Nova, if you'd prefer, but be aware that while smoked salmon is generally pretty safe to eat, these type of preserved fish do carry a Listeria risk. Most healthy adults won't get sick from exposure to the bacteria, but it can be dangerous for the elderly, pregnant women, small children, those undergoing chemotherapy, or people who are immune-compromised. If you're serving anyone for whom Listeria could be a concern, hot-smoked salmon appears to be a safer bet.

# Challah Strata with Mushrooms and Asparagus

SERVES 4 TO 6 | DAIRY

*No one else seems to remember it, but my grandmother served a Cheddar cheese strata once at a brunch when I was a kid. I can still see her bringing it to the dining room table, and I recall asking her what it was. The name stuck with me—I liked the sound of "strata." But it wasn't a standard family recipe, so I didn't really think about it again until many years later, when I was looking for a way to use up leftover challah. This one includes lots of vegetables, and makes a great savory brunch dish or light dinner.*

Prep time: 20 minutes
Cook time: 55 minutes

1 tablespoon butter, plus extra for greasing the baking dish

1 pound challah, cut into 1-inch cubes (about 8 to 9 cups)

1 tablespoon extra-virgin olive oil, plus extra for drizzling

3 large garlic cloves, smashed, peeled, and finely chopped

1 (10-ounce) package cremini mushrooms, cleaned, stemmed, and cut into small wedges

1 large red bell pepper, seeded and chopped

12 asparagus spears, trimmed and chopped into ¼-inch pieces

½ teaspoon sea salt or kosher salt, plus more for seasoning

Freshly ground black pepper

6 large eggs

1½ cups milk

1½ cups shredded mozzarella cheese

5 ounces herbed goat cheese, crumbled

Preheat the oven to 350°F. Butter an 8-by-8-by-2-inch baking dish, or a 2-quart ceramic baking dish. Place the cubed challah into a large bowl and set aside.

In a chef's pan or large skillet set over medium-high heat, warm the butter and olive oil until the butter melts and starts to foam. Add the garlic and sauté for 30 seconds, then stir in the mushrooms and cook, sautéing frequently, until the mushrooms soften and release their juice, about 5 minutes. When most of the liquid in the pan has cooked off, add the bell pepper and asparagus and sauté until the peppers and asparagus are crisp-tender, about 5 minutes more. Remove from the heat, season with salt and black pepper, and set aside to cool.

In a large bowl, whisk together the eggs, milk, and ½ teaspoon salt. Pour over the challah cubes, and gently fold together so all the bread is saturated with the egg mixture. Let stand for 15 minutes so the challah can absorb the custard.

Spoon half the soaked challah into the prepared baking dish, smoothing with a spatula to spread the challah cubes to the edges of the dish. Top evenly with all the vegetables. Sprinkle evenly with half of the shredded mozzarella, then half of the goat cheese.

Top with the remaining challah cubes, smoothing them to the edges of the dish. Sprinkle evenly with the rest of the mozzarella, then goat cheese. Drizzle olive oil on top of the strata.

Bake in the preheated oven until the strata is puffed and golden, and a tester inserted in the center comes out clean, about 40 to 45 minutes. Allow to rest for a few minutes before serving.

STORAGE: *Leftover strata may be stored, covered, in the refrigerator for up to 2 days. Reheat before serving.*

Simple Swap

Try swapping other favorite cheeses for the mozzarella and goat cheese. You can also add finely chopped fresh herbs, such as basil, chives, or dill, to the egg mixture.

# Poppy-Topped Cheddar Quiche

SERVES 6 TO 8 | DAIRY

*For as long as I can remember, this crustless Cheddar quiche has made an appearance at family brunches, Yom Kippur break fasts, and casual dinners. It was a recipe shared among my grandmother and her friends, and was no doubt clipped by one of them from a Bisquick advertisement decades ago. My grandmother liked to serve it when she hosted the ladies for their "Stitch and Chatter Club" sessions; they'd converge around her dining room table with cross-stitch, crochet, and embroidery projects, and while away the afternoon together over handiwork, gossip, and good food.*

*Prep time: 20 minutes*
*Cook time: 1 hour*

4 tablespoons unsalted butter

1 large sweet onion, peeled and chopped
(or 1 cup frozen chopped onions)

1½ cups all-purpose buttermilk baking mix,
such as Bisquick

1½ cups milk

1 large egg

2 cups grated Cheddar cheese

1 tablespoon poppy seeds

Preheat the oven to 350°F. Lightly grease a 10½-inch quiche dish, a 9-inch ovenproof pie dish, or an 8-inch-square baking pan.

In a large skillet or sauté pan set over medium heat, melt the butter. Add the onions and sauté until soft and translucent, about 5 to 7 minutes. Remove the pan from the heat and set aside to cool slightly.

In a large bowl, whisk together the baking mix, milk, and egg just until smooth. Stir in a spoonful of the onions (this will temper the batter and keep the egg from curdling). Add the rest of the onions and butter from the skillet, and mix well. Stir in the grated cheese.

Pour the mixture into the prepared baking dish, and smooth the top with a spatula. Sprinkle the quiche evenly with the poppy seeds.

Bake in the preheated oven for 50 minutes to 1 hour, until the quiche is set in the center, golden and crusty near the edges, and a tester inserted in the center comes out fairly clean.

Cool slightly on a rack for 5 to 10 minutes before serving.

# Three-Cheese Quiche with Caramelized Onions and Spinach

SERVES 6 TO 8 | DAIRY

*Over the years, we've tried lots of vegetable additions to my grandmother's quiche, with delicious results. But my attempts to replace the Bisquick with a more whole-some whole-grain (or at least additive-free) blend always fell flat. I was about to try again, when I thought of family and friends with celiac disease and realized it would be nice to have a gluten-free quiche in my repertoire. Plus, by keeping the recipe totally grain-free, it's a natural fit for Passover entertaining too.*

*Prep time: 20 minutes*
*Cook time: 1 hour, 15 minutes*

2 tablespoons unsalted butter, plus extra for greasing the baking dish

1 large onion, peeled and chopped

1 tablespoon extra-virgin olive oil

1 (10-ounce) package frozen chopped spinach or broccoli

4 large eggs

1 cup milk

¼ teaspoon sea salt or kosher salt

Freshly ground black pepper

1 cup grated Cheddar cheese

1 cup grated fontina cheese

1 small red bell pepper, cored, seeded, and thinly cut into strips

2 tablespoons grated Parmesan cheese

Preheat the oven to 400°F. Lightly butter a 9-inch glass ovenproof pie dish.

In a large skillet set over medium-high heat, melt the butter. Add the onions and cook, sautéing frequently, until they soften and begin to caramelize, about 10 to 12 minutes. Transfer the onions to a large bowl.

In the same pan, warm the olive oil, then add the spinach or broccoli. Sauté until the vegetables are cooked through and any moisture has evaporated. Transfer to the bowl with the onions.

In a medium bowl, whisk together the eggs, milk, and salt until the mixture is a uniform pale lemon color. Season with a few grinds of black pepper, and whisk to combine. Slowly pour the egg mixture into the large bowl with the vegetable mixture, while simultaneously stirring to combine. Add the Cheddar and fontina cheeses, and mix well. *(CONTINUED)*

Pour the mixture into the buttered pie dish. Arrange the pepper strips decoratively on top of the quiche.

Bake in the preheated oven for 35 minutes. Sprinkle evenly with the Parmesan, and bake for 10 to 20 minutes more, or until the quiche is set in the center and a tester comes out clean. Remove from the oven and allow to rest for a few minutes before serving.

STORAGE: *Leftover quiche may be stored, covered, in the refrigerator for 1 to 2 days. Reheat, covered in foil, in a preheated 300°F oven.*

# Pecan and Walnut Sticky Buns

MAKES 12 STICKY BUNS | DAIRY

*The Settlement Cookbook was my grandmother's primary culinary reference. And the most worn, splattered page was the one with the recipe for rich kuchen dough. She multiplied the recipe to make copious quantities of butter horns—hand-rolled crescent cookies filled with crushed walnuts and sugar. I wanted to work with the dough, but not to fuss with dozens upon dozens of cookies. Cinnamon rolls seemed a less fussy option, but when I tasted Aunt Esther's pecan kugel (reimagined on page 44), I was inspired to turn them into sticky buns. The walnuts are a nod to my grandmother's butter horn filling, and add dimension to the usual pecan topping. I like to enrich the buns with whole-wheat flour, but you can use all-purpose only for a more classic dough.*

*Prep time: 35 minutes*
*Rising time: 2 ½ hours, or 1 hour*
*then overnight*
*Cook time: 35 minutes*

### FOR THE DOUGH

1 ½ cups all-purpose flour, plus extra
   as needed

1 cup white whole-wheat flour

½ teaspoon fine sea salt

1 ⅛ teaspoons (½ packet) active dry yeast

2 tablespoons warm water

½ cup (1 stick) unsalted butter

¼ cup sugar

1 large egg

Zest of ¼ lemon

½ cup milk

### FOR THE FILLING

2 tablespoons butter, melted

⅓ cup brown sugar

1 ½ tablespoons cinnamon

½ cup raisins

### FOR THE TOPPING

½ cup (1 stick) unsalted butter, melted

¼ cup brown sugar

¼ cup pure maple syrup, preferably dark

⅓ cup chopped walnuts

⅓ cup chopped pecans

*(CONTINUED)*

MAKE THE DOUGH: In a medium bowl, whisk together the all-purpose flour, whole-wheat flour, and salt. Set aside.

In a small bowl, combine the yeast and warm water. Allow to sit until it begins to bubble and foam, about 5 to 10 minutes. If the yeast is not reactive, discard it and start with fresh yeast.

In a large bowl or a stand mixer fitted with a whisk or paddle attachment, cream together the butter and sugar. Add the egg and lemon zest, and beat on medium speed until the mixture is a light lemon yellow color. Add the milk and yeast mixture, and beat on low to combine. If you are using a stand mixer, switch to the dough hook. Slowly add the flour and mix with a sturdy spoon or the mixer until the flour is incorporated and the dough begins to pull into a ball. If it is very sticky, add additional flour, 1 tablespoon at a time, mixing well after each addition. The dough should be smooth, soft, and slightly tacky, but shouldn't be too sticky to handle.

Knead in the mixer on low speed for 5 minutes, or by hand on a lightly floured surface for 5 to 10 minutes. If you kneaded by hand, return the dough to the bowl. If you let the mixer knead, simply remove the bowl from the machine. Cover the bowl with plastic wrap or a tea towel, and allow the dough to rise in a warm place until doubled in bulk, about 1 hour.

When the dough has risen, punch it down. On a lightly floured surface, pat it into a square, then roll it out into a rectangle about 10-by-15 inches.

MAKE THE FILLING: Brush the dough with the melted butter. Sprinkle evenly with brown sugar, leaving a 1-inch border at one long end. Sprinkle with the cinnamon, then the raisins. Starting at the long end without the border, tightly roll up the dough, jellyroll-style. Let the roll rest, seam side down, while you prepare the topping.

MAKE THE TOPPING: Pour the melted butter into a 9-by-9-by-2-inch baking pan, and spread to cover the bottom. Sprinkle evenly with the brown sugar, then drizzle with the maple syrup. Sprinkle evenly with the walnuts and pecans.

With a sharp knife, slice the rolled-up dough crosswise into 12 even pieces. Lay the pieces, cut side up, on top of the nut topping in the baking pan. Don't worry if a little space remains in the pan—that will give the buns room to rise. Cover the pan with plastic wrap.

If you plan to bake the buns the same day, allow to rise in a warm place for 1 to 1½ hours, or until they've expanded to mostly fill the pan. To bake the next day, cover the pan with plastic wrap and place in the refrigerator, where they will slowly rise overnight.

When you are ready to bake, preheat the oven to 375°F. If the buns were in the refrigerator, allow them to rest at room temperature until the oven is hot. (Refrigerated buns may not rise enough to fill the pan overnight, but will expand while baking.) Place the pan in the oven and bake until the buns are puffed and a deep golden brown color, and a tester inserted near the center comes out clean of dough, about 30 to 35 minutes. Remove the pan from the oven and place on a wire rack to cool for about 10 to 15 minutes. Invert the pan over a serving platter and serve warm.

STORAGE: *The sticky buns are best eaten fresh from the oven, but can be kept, after cooling, well-wrapped in parchment and foil, for 1 day. For longer storage, place the wrapped buns in a zipper-top freezer bag and store for up to 3 months. Reheat the buns in a 300°F oven until warm and tender. Let cool slightly before eating—the topping will be hot!*

Note

Since you'll be using the zest, seek out organic lemons for this recipe. Pesticide residues tend to concentrate in the skins of citrus fruits, and non-organic lemons are more likely to be waxed. If you can't find organic fruit, scrub your lemon well before zesting.

# Pecan-Topped Cherry Ricotta Kugel

SERVES 10 TO 12 | DAIRY

*My grandmother and her beloved sister, Rose, made sweet dairy kugels, and both loved ice cream, so I created a cherry vanilla kugel in their honor. When I discovered a pecan kugel found in my Aunt Esther's recipe stash shortly after she passed away, I made it as an homage to Bubbe, her mother. Both were destined for this book, but each was missing something. So on a whim, I married the two recipes, and came up with a much better one. I love that the new recipe pays tribute to the women on both sides of the family, while taking a fresh turn.*

**Prep time: 15 minutes**
**Cook time: 1 hour**

### FOR THE TOPPING

4 tablespoons unsalted butter, melted

½ cup packed dark brown sugar

1 cup pecan halves and pieces

### FOR THE KUGEL

1 (12-ounce) package wide egg noodles

6 tablespoons unsalted butter, cut into
    small pieces

1 (16-ounce) container sour cream

1 (15-ounce) container ricotta

¾ cup sugar

4 large eggs, lightly beaten

1 tablespoon vanilla extract

¼ teaspoon fine sea salt

1 cup fresh or frozen pitted cherries,
    dried tart cherries, or a mix

**MAKE THE TOPPING:** Add the melted butter to a 9-by-13-by-2-inch glass or ceramic baking dish, tilting the pan to cover the bottom with butter. Sprinkle evenly with the brown sugar, then pecans. Set aside.

**MAKE THE KUGEL:** Preheat the oven to 350°F. Bring a large pot of water to a boil. Add the egg noodles and cook for 5 to 7 minutes, or until they begin to turn tender. Drain and place in a large bowl. Add the butter to the hot noodles and stir until it coats the noodles evenly.

Add the sour cream, ricotta, and sugar to the noodles and mix well. Add the eggs, vanilla, and salt, and mix again, until the eggs are fully integrated into the noodle mixture. Fold in the cherries.

Pour the noodle mixture into the prepared pan. Cover with foil and bake for 40 minutes. Remove the foil and bake for 10 to 15 minutes more, or until the kugel is set, the top is golden, and a tester inserted in the center comes out fairly clean. Remove the kugel from the oven and cool on a wire rack for 10 to 15 minutes before cutting.

# Blueberry Oat Scones

MAKES 8 SCONES | DAIRY

*My grandmother Ruth loved blueberries, and used them in everything from muffins to blintzes to pies. As a kid, I preferred them fresh, but lately I've taken a shine to them in baked goods and smoothies. In these whole-grain oat scones, the juicy bursts of berry are the perfect counterpoint to the hearty grains.*

**Prep time: 10 minutes**
**Cook time: 22 minutes**

1 cup white whole-wheat flour

1 cup old-fashioned rolled oats

¼ cup sugar

1 tablespoon plus 1 teaspoon baking powder

¼ teaspoon fine sea salt

¼ teaspoon ground ginger

6 tablespoons butter, melted

⅓ cup milk

1 large egg

1 cup fresh or frozen blueberries

**STORAGE:** *The scones are best the same day they're made, but will keep for a day at room temperature wrapped in foil. For extended storage, wrap in foil, place in a zipper-top freezer bag, and freeze for up to 2 months. Reheat the scones in a 300°F oven before serving.*

Preheat the oven to 400°F. Line a rimmed baking sheet with parchment paper or a silicone liner.

In a large bowl, whisk together the flour, oats, sugar, baking powder, salt, and ginger.

Add the melted butter and milk and stir to combine. Add the egg and mix well, just until the mixture is lump-free. Fold in the blueberries.

Turn out the dough onto a lightly floured surface and shape into a disc about 8-inches wide by 2-inches thick. Use a large knife to cut the dough into 8 wedges.

Bake in the preheated oven for 18 to 22 minutes, or until puffed and golden.

### Simple Swap

Instead of blueberries, you can substitute ⅛ cup of dried fruit, such as currants, raisins, or chopped dried cherries.

# Apricot Pistachio Babka

SERVES 10 TO 12 | PAREVE

*Babka is having a major moment, and why not? There's lots to love about the loaves of twisted dough, generously interspersed with a filling that usually involves lots of chocolate. Many professional bakers behind babka's renaissance are working with laminated doughs—yeasted dairy doughs turned with lots of butter. I thought about doing the same, but the challenge of creating a delicious pareve babka made without margarine won out. I couldn't shake thoughts of my grandmother's love of apricots, so I built the filling around them. I love the cheeky marriage of Sephardic flavors wrapped in a quintessentially Ashkenazi pastry.*

*Prep time: 50 minutes*
*Rising time: 2 ½ to 3 hours, or 1 hour then overnight*
*Cook time: 50 minutes*

### FOR THE DOUGH

½ cup soy milk, gently warmed

1⅛ teaspoons (½ packet) active dry yeast

1½ cups all-purpose flour, plus 2 to 4 tablespoons more if needed

1 cup white whole-wheat flour

¼ cup sugar

½ teaspoon fine sea salt

3 tablespoons virgin coconut oil

2 tablespoons neutral oil, such as canola or grapeseed

1 large egg

### FOR THE FILLING

1 cup tart dried apricots

¼ cup golden raisins

⅓ cup dry-roasted, unsalted, shelled pistachios

¼ cup sugar

2 teaspoons virgin coconut oil

½ teaspoon cinnamon

½ teaspoon ground ginger

### FOR THE TOPPING

4 tablespoons all-purpose flour

1½ tablespoons sugar

1 teaspoon cinnamon

1 tablespoon neutral oil, such as canola or grapeseed

*(CONTINUED)*

FIG. 1    FIG. 2    FIG. 3

MAKE THE DOUGH: In a stand mixer fitted with a dough hook, or a large bowl, combine the soy milk and yeast. Allow to stand until foamy, 5 to 10 minutes.

In another bowl, whisk together the flours, sugar, and salt. Add to the yeast mixture, mixing with a wooden spoon or the mixer's dough hook on medium speed. Add the coconut oil and canola or grapeseed oil, and continue beating until incorporated. Add the egg and mix until the dough begins to pull into a ball.

Knead with the dough hook for 5 minutes, or by hand on a lightly floured surface for 5 to 10 minutes, until the dough is slightly tacky but smooth. If the dough is very sticky, knead in the additional flour, 1 tablespoon at a time, just until the dough is no longer too sticky to handle. If you kneaded by hand, return the dough to the bowl. If you let the mixer knead, simply remove the bowl from the machine. Cover the bowl with a clean tea towel or plastic wrap and allow the dough to rise until doubled, about 1 to 1½ hours.

MAKE THE FILLING: While the dough is rising, place the apricots and raisins in separate bowls, add enough warm water to cover, and soak for about 10 minutes or until soft. Drain each separately, pat dry, and return to the bowls.

Place the pistachios in the work bowl of a food processor, and pulse several times to grind to a fine flour. If you don't have a food processor, use a mortar and pestle. Or chop the pistachios finely with a knife, then crush with a rolling pin. Transfer the pulverized pistachios to a small dish and set aside.

Next, place the apricots, sugar, coconut oil, cinnamon, and ginger into the work bowl of the food processor (it's fine if some pistachio residue remains). Pulse several times, until a smooth paste forms. To make the filling by hand, chop the apricots as finely as possible, place in a bowl with the other ingredients, and use your hands to mix and knead the filling into as smooth a paste as you can.

FIG. 4

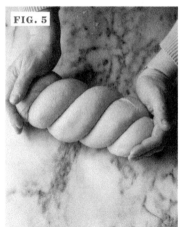

FIG. 5

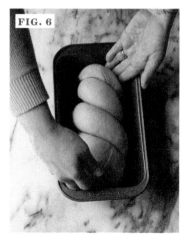

FIG. 6

Grease a 9-by-5-by-2½-inch loaf pan. When the dough has risen, punch it down and divide it in half. Pat each piece of dough into a rectangle. On a lightly floured surface, roll one portion of dough into a 9-by-15-inch rectangle about ¼-inch thick (Fig. 1). Spread with half the apricot filling, leaving a 1-inch border along one of the long sides. Sprinkle evenly with half the ground pistachios, then half the raisins (Fig. 2). Starting on the long side without the border, roll the dough up tightly, jellyroll-style (Fig. 3). Pinch the ends together gently to seal. Allow the roll to rest, seam side down, while you repeat the process with the other piece of dough and the remaining filling.

Lay the rolls side by side, seam sides down. Starting in the middle, twist the rolls together by laying one over the other until you get to the ends (Fig. 4). Gently compress the ends between your hands to shorten the loaf enough to fit it into the loaf pan (Figs. 5 and 6). Cover the pan with a clean tea towel or plastic wrap and allow to rise in a warm place until the babka mostly fills the pan, about 1½ to 2 hours.

(If you'd prefer, you can also cover the pan with plastic and refrigerate overnight. You will need to bring the babka to room temperature before baking.)

MAKE THE TOPPING: First, preheat the oven to 350°F, as you'll want to place the babka in the oven immediately after putting on the topping. In a small bowl, whisk together the flour, sugar, and cinnamon. Stir in the oil until the flour mixture is moistened and small lumps form. Sprinkle the topping over the babka. Place the loaf pan on a piece of foil on the center rack of the oven (the foil will catch any bits of crumb topping that may fall off). Bake in the preheated oven, turning the pan after 30 minutes, until the babka is golden and firm to the touch, about 45 to 50 minutes total. Remove from the oven and transfer to a wire rack to cool.

STORAGE: *The babka will keep, well wrapped at room temperature, for 5 days. Or wrap well in foil, place in a plastic freezer bag, and freeze for up to 2 months.*

# Sour Cream and Banana Muffins

MAKES 12 MUFFINS | DAIRY

*I used to sit in the orange vinyl chair at my grandmother's white Formica kitchen table, while she stood at the counter slicing bananas, or sometimes strawberries, into a bowl. She'd top them with a dollop of sour cream, sprinkle them with sugar, and bring the bowl to me. I'd mix everything up, and then we'd snack. This was one of her ultimate comfort foods, and sparked the idea for these muffins. If you're sitting down to breakfast, they'd be nice served alongside their simple inspiration.*

*Prep time: 15 minutes*
*Cook time: 25 minutes*

FOR THE STREUSEL TOPPING

¼ cup packed brown sugar

¼ cup white whole-wheat flour

1 teaspoon cinnamon

2 tablespoons cold unsalted butter,
    cut into small pieces

FOR THE MUFFINS

1 cup all-purpose flour

1 cup white whole-wheat flour

1½ teaspoons baking powder

¼ teaspoon baking soda

¼ teaspoon fine sea salt

1 cup sour cream

6 tablespoons unsalted butter, melted

½ cup sugar

2 teaspoons pure vanilla extract

1 large egg

1 cup mashed ripe banana (2 to 3 bananas)

Preheat the oven to 375°F. Line a 12-cup muffin tin with paper liners, or grease and flour the cups.

**MAKE THE STREUSEL TOPPING:** In a small bowl, mix the brown sugar, flour, and cinnamon. Rub the butter into the sugar–flour mixture with your fingers until small clumps form. Set aside.

**MAKE THE MUFFINS:** In a large bowl, whisk together the flours, baking powder, baking soda, and salt.

In another large bowl, mix the sour cream, butter, sugar, and vanilla. Whisk in the egg, then the banana.

Add the wet ingredients to the dry ingredients and mix well, just until the batter is smooth and lump-free.

Spoon the mixture into the muffin cups, filling each cup about ¾ full. Top each muffin with streusel. Bake in the preheated oven for 22 to 25 minutes, or until the muffins are puffed, firm, and golden, and a cake tester inserted in the center comes out clean. Place the muffin tin on a rack to cool.

# Passover Pancakes

MAKES 12 TO 16 PANCAKES | DAIRY

*I've always liked my grandmother's Passover pancakes well enough. But I never escaped the feeling they were mostly meant to change things up from a steady breakfast of matzo brei (fried matzo, the holiday's delectable answer to French toast)—which, frankly, I much preferred. In the last several years, though, certain kosher for Passover products that've hit the market have proved game changers in the pancake department. Specifically, when I found tapioca starch, baking powder, and legit vanilla extract, I snatched them up. But the bubbes of the world didn't have these novel Pesach ingredients, so I had no idea what to do with them, other than make pancakes. Turns out that was a pretty good idea.*

*Prep time: 10 minutes*
*Cook time: 15 minutes*

¾ cup matzo cake meal

¼ cup tapioca starch

1 tablespoon sugar

1 teaspoon kosher for Passover baking powder

1⅓ cups milk

2 large eggs, lightly beaten

2 tablespoons unsalted butter, melted

1 teaspoon pure vanilla extract

Oil or butter for the pan

Jam, fruit, cinnamon, sugar, and/or pure maple syrup, for serving

### Simple Swap

If you can't find tapioca starch, potato starch works too. The texture won't have quite the same chew, but the pancakes will still be tasty!

Preheat the oven to 200°F. Line a baking dish or sheet pan with parchment paper, or keep an oven-proof serving platter close at hand.

In a large bowl, whisk together the matzo cake meal, tapioca starch, sugar, and baking powder.

Make a well in the dry ingredients. Add the milk, eggs, melted butter, and vanilla. Mix well, just until the batter is smooth and lump-free.

Warm a large cast iron or nonstick skillet over medium-high heat. Add a little oil or butter and spread around to cover the bottom of the skillet. Drop the batter by large spoonfuls into the skillet (you'll be able to make 3 to 4 pancakes at a time, depending on the size of your skillet).

*(CONTINUED)*

Cook for 1 to 2 minutes, or until the edges are set and bubbles form on the surface. With a wide, thin spatula, carefully flip the pancakes. Cook for 1 to 2 minutes more, or until golden brown on both sides.

Transfer the pancakes to baking dish or platter, tent with foil, and slide into the preheated oven to keep warm while you make the rest of the pancakes.

Serve with jam, cinnamon, and sugar, or pure maple syrup.

STORAGE: *Leftover pancakes can be wrapped in foil and stored in the refrigerator for 1 to 2 days. Reheat in a 300°F oven.*

# IN THE KITCHEN WITH
# PAULA SHOYER

*I trace the start of my career to the first time I watched my grandmother, Sylvia Altman, measure cake ingredients with her hands. The only time I saw her use a mixer was to beat egg whites. Otherwise she mixed by hand well into her early nineties.*

*There was never a recipe in sight, and yet her yeast cake, rugelach, and brownies came out perfect every time. And although I bake from recipes, I learned from her to trust my instincts while making a recipe, to add a little more flour to soft dough and to oil my hands when shaping drier dough.*

*I grew up in the 1970s and was encouraged to pursue medicine, law, or education, and never knew that baking was something I could do professionally. Even Grandma was skeptical when I started pastry school in Paris. She said, "Who goes to school to learn how to bake a cake? You just bake a cake!" And when people started paying me for desserts, she wondered if maybe she should have been selling hers all along.*

*Grandma never saw my three cookbooks, but in 2011 I was invited to do a cooking demonstration for a synagogue in Brooklyn and the rabbi was living in Grandma's former house. When they contacted me, they had no idea that I had a connection to the house. I taught the class in the same kitchen where I first developed my love of baking. When I started to speak, I thought I would be weepy, as Grandma was gone. But I found that at that moment, I knew I was exactly where I was meant to be, doing precisely what I was meant to be doing with my life.*

**PAULA SHOYER**, known as The Kosher Baker, is the author of *The Kosher Baker*, *The Holiday Kosher Baker*, and *The New Passover Menu*.

*Clockwise from top:* Za'atar Pita Chips (page 69), Feta and Olives with Oregano (page 72), Muhammara (page 62), Smoky Spice-Roasted Chickpeas (page 59)

# CHAPTER THREE

# Mezze and Snacks

My grandmother was always ready to entertain. Bowls brimming with nuts and candy had perpetual spots on sideboards and end tables. Tucked into the pantry or freezer were nice cookies, ready to be pulled out at a moment's notice should an unexpected guest happen to drop by. (God forbid a friend should stop in and leave hungry!) The lesson I gleaned was that playing host ought to be more about hospitality than arduous preparation. With a repertoire of simple go-to snacks (along with a showstopper or two), enjoying company—or just a quiet evening kicking back with the family—is a very doable proposition.

# Moroccan-Spiced Carrot Dip

MAKES ABOUT 1 ½ CUPS | PAREVE

*Though she was incredibly nurturing, my grandmother didn't believe in baby talk any more than she saw the sense in a children's menu. She believed that even infants could understand language, and deserved to be spoken to normally. And she offered the same food to all—even if she'd slip the kids an extra cookie. Plenty of nutrition research bears out the wisdom behind offering little ones the same food the family eats. And despite the American tendency to eschew all spices in baby food, newbie eaters often savor a little seasoning. Though this carrot dip was designed as grown-up party fare, my kids liked it from babyhood.*

*Prep time: 10 minutes*
*Cook time: 15 minutes*

1 pound carrots, peeled and cut into
    1-inch chunks

¼ cup water

2 to 3 garlic cloves, peeled and finely chopped

¾ teaspoon peeled and grated fresh ginger

½ teaspoon paprika

¼ teaspoon cinnamon

¼ teaspoon ground coriander

2 teaspoons freshly squeezed lemon juice

2 tablespoons extra-virgin olive oil

Freshly chopped parsley for garnish
    (optional)

In a small saucepan, combine the carrots and water. Bring to a boil over medium-high heat, reduce to low, cover, and cook for about 15 minutes, or until the carrots are very tender.

Using a food processor or immersion blender, purée the carrots. Add the garlic, ginger, paprika, cinnamon, coriander, and lemon juice, and purée until smooth. Drizzle in the olive oil, and pulse to blend.

Transfer to a serving dish. Just before serving, garnish with freshly chopped parsley, if using. Serve warm or at room temperature with pita chips, baguette slices, or crudités.

**STORAGE:** *Store leftover carrot dip, covered, in the refrigerator for up to 3 days.*

# Deviled Eggs with Chives and Smoked Paprika

SERVES 10 TO 12 | PAREVE

*As kids are wont to do, I abruptly decided I hated eggs at some point in my youth. I refused to eat anything perceptibly eggy until I was in college, when omelets just as suddenly seemed appealing again. But I never stopped loving the look of the deviled eggs that my grandmother and my mom would make for parties and brunches. They managed to seem fancy and cute at once, with their chive-flecked yolks and jaunty sprinkle of sweet paprika. Now I favor them dusted with smoked paprika, and served with cocktails.*

*Prep time: 25 minutes*
*Cook time: 15 minutes*

12 large eggs
¼ to ½ cup mayonnaise
2 teaspoons Dijon mustard
1 tablespoon fresh snipped chives, or
    1½ teaspoons dried chives
Smoked or sweet paprika

Place the eggs in a pot large enough to hold them in a single layer. If necessary, use 2 pots. Add enough cold water to cover the eggs by 1 inch.

Place the pot(s) over medium-high heat and cook, uncovered, until the water comes to a rolling boil. Cover, remove from the heat, and let the eggs sit in the water for 15 minutes.

While the eggs are cooking, prepare an ice bath by filling a large bowl with ice and cold water.

When the eggs are ready, use a slotted spoon to carefully transfer them to the ice bath. Allow the eggs to sit in the cold water for 15 minutes to cool.

After cooling, gently crack the eggs and roll them on a countertop, then peel. If the shells cling, try peeling them under cold running water. Halve the eggs lengthwise. Carefully remove the yolks and place them in a medium bowl. Place the whites on a platter and set aside.

With a wire whisk or fork, mash the yolks. Stir in ¼ cup mayonnaise, and continue mashing the yolks until smooth. Stir in the mustard and taste. If you prefer a creamier texture or milder flavor, add up to ¼ cup additional mayonnaise, 1 tablespoon at a time, mixing after each addition. Stir in the chives.

Transfer the yolk mixture into a pastry bag and pipe into the hollows of the egg whites. Or simply spoon the yolks into the egg whites. Refrigerate, covered, until ready to serve. Just before serving, dust with paprika.

STORAGE: *Leftover deviled eggs will keep, covered, in the refrigerator for up to 2 days.*

# Smoky Spice-Roasted Chickpeas

SERVES 4 | PAREVE

*The deviled eggs that my grandmother prepared (and certain other recipes, like her matzo balls with parsley and nutmeg, on page 131) taught me the magic of using a little spice to bump up the flavor and stamp a personal signature on favorite dishes. Smoked paprika adds amazing depth to the spice blend on these crisp-on-the-outside, tender-on-the-inside, absolutely crave-worthy chickpeas.*

*Prep time: 5 minutes*
*Cook time: 20 minutes*

1 (15-ounce) can chickpeas, drained and rinsed

1 teaspoon ground cumin

1 teaspoon garlic powder

½ teaspoon smoked paprika

¼ teaspoon sea salt or kosher salt

1 tablespoon extra-virgin olive oil

### Note

While these are delicious eaten out of hand with a cold beer or cocktail, they're also an incredibly versatile accent. Try them strewn over hummus or other dips, mixed into grain salads, rolled into wraps, or served atop green salads.

Preheat the oven to 425°F. Pat the chickpeas dry with a clean tea towel or paper towel. Place them in a single layer on a small rimmed baking sheet or in a 9-by-9-by-2-inch metal baking pan.

Sprinkle the chickpeas evenly with the cumin, garlic powder, smoked paprika, and salt. With a spoon or clean hands, toss the chickpeas to coat with the spices. Drizzle with the olive oil, and toss again.

Roast in the preheated oven for about 20 minutes, shaking the pan a couple of times during cooking, until the chickpeas are crisp and golden outside and tender inside. Spoon into a serving bowl and serve warm with drinks.

# Patacones with Simple Guacamole

SERVES 2 TO 4 | PAREVE

*When we returned from winter break one year during college, my friends and I found ourselves collectively bummed out by the prospect of eating cafeteria food after a month of home cooking. So we commandeered the unused dorm kitchen and spent the rest of the year making dinner together. We ate pasta and salad nearly every night, but made the sauce and vinaigrette from scratch, using our French/Israeli/Turkish friend's mom's recipes. A vegan, the child of hippies, taught us to roll maki; a friend from Japan perfected our technique. And our Colombian friend taught us to make patacones—that is, smashed plantain chips—which we'd fry up and share to assuage bouts of homesickness.*

*Prep time: 15 minutes*
*Cook time: 20 minutes*

### FOR THE GUACAMOLE

1 large, ripe avocado, halved lengthwise and pitted
1 to 2 garlic cloves, peeled, smashed, and finely chopped
Juice of ½ large lemon, plus more for serving

### FOR THE PATACONES

2 green plantains
Neutral oil, such as canola or grapeseed
Kosher salt or sea salt

**MAKE THE GUACAMOLE:** Score the avocado flesh into ½-inch cubes, then scoop it from its skin into a medium bowl. Smash the avocado with a fork, add the garlic and lemon juice, and mix well. Taste and add more lemon juice or garlic if desired. Set aside.

**MAKE THE PATACONES:** Line a couple of large plates with paper towels. Cut the ends off of the plantains, and run a sharp knife lengthwise through the skin, taking care not to cut into the fruit inside. Pull away the skin, and slice the plantains crosswise into 1-inch-thick rounds.

In a large, deep skillet (cast iron is ideal), heat about 1 inch of oil over medium-high heat until it shimmers. Working in batches, carefully slip several plantain slices into the hot oil, and fry, turning once, until they begin to turn golden, about 3 to 4 minutes. Transfer the plantains to the towel-lined plates to drain while you finish frying the slices. When all of the plantains have been transferred to the towel-lined plates, turn off the heat but don't discard the oil.

As the fried plantains turn cool enough to handle, place them, one at a time, in the center of a saucer or small plate. Top with a second saucer or plate, and press down to flatten the plantains to about ¼-inch thickness. Repeat with the rest of the plantains.

Reheat the oil in the skillet, and when it is hot, add the flattened plantains to the oil and fry again until both sides are golden brown and the patacones are crisp on the outside, about 3 to 4 minutes more.

Transfer to towel-lined plates to remove the excess oil, sprinkle with salt, and serve immediately with the guacamole.

STORAGE: *The patacones should be eaten immediately, but you can make the guacamole several hours in advance and store, covered, in the refrigerator. Bury the pit in the guacamole to help prevent browning. Leftover guacamole can be refrigerated for 1 to 2 days, though the surface will tend to turn brown.*

# Muhammara

MAKES ABOUT 2 CUPS | PAREVE

*When a friend gave my mom the recipe for this classic roasted pepper and walnut dip, popular throughout the Levant, it quickly became a favorite for entertaining. Delicious with fresh, warm pita and crudités, it's also great in wraps or dolloped on grilled fish or chicken.*

*Prep time: 10 minutes*

1 cup roasted red peppers

⅔ cup fresh bread crumbs

½ cup walnuts

2 large garlic cloves, smashed and finely chopped

1 tablespoon freshly squeezed lemon juice

1 tablespoon pomegranate molasses (optional)

1 teaspoon ground cumin

½ teaspoon red pepper flakes

3 tablespoons extra-virgin olive oil

In the work bowl of a food processor or the jar of a blender, combine the roasted red peppers, bread crumbs, walnuts, garlic, lemon juice, pomegranate molasses (if using), cumin, and red pepper flakes. Pulse several times to blend.

With the processor or blender running, slowly pour the olive oil through the feed tube, and purée until the mixture is smooth. Transfer the muhammara to a serving bowl.

STORAGE: *Muhammara may be stored, covered, in the refrigerator for 2 to 3 days.*

Tip

If you don't have pomegranate molasses, balsamic vinegar makes a good substitute.

# Thai Summer Rolls with Peanut Sauce

SERVES 4 TO 6 | PAREVE

*My grandmother was entranced by Thailand. She loved the art, dance, and architecture.* The King and I *was one of her favorite musicals, despite its debatable historical accuracy. She traveled there with my grandfather, and brought back art, jewelry, silks, and cutlery that remain family treasures. Even while traveling overseas, she upheld the principles of a kosher diet. I imagine she would have dined on things like these cold vegetarian summer rolls, and would have surely replicated them back at home, if only she could have gotten her hands on the ingredients.*

*Prep time: 30 minutes*

### FOR THE PEANUT SAUCE

- 2 tablespoons smooth peanut butter (preferably natural)
- 1 tablespoon brown sugar
- 2 tablespoons hot water
- 2 tablespoons unseasoned rice vinegar
- 2 tablespoons tamari soy sauce (reduced sodium is fine)
- 1 tablespoon freshly squeezed lime juice (from about ½ lime)
- 1 teaspoon sriracha or hot sauce

### FOR THE SUMMER ROLLS

- 8 (8-inch diameter) dried rice paper wrappers
- 1 small head of Boston or gem lettuce, leaves rinsed and patted dry
- 1 medium red bell pepper, cored, seeded, and cut into thin strips
- 1 medium cucumber, peeled, seeded, and cut into matchsticks
- 1 large carrot, peeled and cut into matchsticks
- 16 fresh mint leaves, rinsed and patted dry

**MAKE THE PEANUT SAUCE:** In a medium bowl, stir the peanut butter and brown sugar together. Stir in the hot water, mixing well to thin and lighten the peanut butter mixture. Add the vinegar, tamari, lime juice, and sriracha or hot sauce, and mix well. Transfer to a serving dish and set aside.

**MAKE THE SUMMER ROLLS:** Cover a serving platter with a slightly damp tea towel, and set aside. Fill a large bowl with warm water. Cover a large cutting board or work surface with a clean tea towel or paper towels.

Take a rice paper round and gently submerge it in the warm water just until it is pliable, about 10 to 15 seconds. Remove from the water, allow any excess water to drip off, then place on the towel-lined work surface.

Lay a lettuce leaf near the bottom half of the rice paper round, tearing the lettuce if it is too large to fit. Top the lettuce with 2 or 3 pepper strips, and a few cucumber and carrot sticks. Top evenly with 2 torn mint leaves.

Starting with the vegetable side, roll up the rice paper just enough to cover the vegetables. Fold the ends in, then continue rolling. Leave whole, or cut in half crosswise if preferred. Place on the serving platter and cover lightly with the damp tea towel.

Repeat the process to make the rest of the summer rolls. Serve immediately with the peanut sauce for dipping. Or cover and refrigerate for up to 4 hours before serving.

Did You Know?

While kosher-certified rice paper wrappers are available, they can be hard to find. But many kosher authorities hold that rice paper and rice noodles containing only rice, water, salt, and tapioca starch don't require special certification. Check with your rabbi or a kosher certification agency if you have any questions about the kosher status of rice paper.

# Potato Cakes with Quick Salted Cod (Coddies)

MAKES 14 TO 18 CODDIES | DAIRY

*The "coddie" is a Baltimore phenomenon dating from at least the early 1900s. Despite the name, there was far more potato than cod in the fried croquettes, which were eaten sandwiched between saltines with a squirt of yellow mustard. Once available on the cheap at soda fountains, delis, diners, and pharmacy luncheonettes, they've practically disappeared today. But when my sister and I were little, they were still ubiquitous enough that my grandmother would grab a few for us to eat by the pool at her apartment complex. Because of my generous use of cod, mine aren't terribly authentic, but they are tasty. And when I added Old Bay to the mix, I finally hit on the seasoning I remembered from childhood.*

*Prep time: 20 minutes*
*Cook time: 35 minutes*

1 (6- to 8-ounce ) cod fillet

Kosher salt

2 medium russet or Yukon gold potatoes, peeled and cut into 1-inch pieces (about 1¼ pounds)

2 tablespoons milk

1½ teaspoons Old Bay seasoning

2 tablespoons chopped fresh parsley

1 tablespoon extra-virgin olive oil, plus more for frying

1 tablespoon unsalted butter, at room temperature

2 large eggs, lightly beaten

¼ to ½ cup soda cracker crumbs

Preheat the oven to 400°F. Rinse the cod and pat dry. Place the cod in a small baking dish and sprinkle on all sides with a generous layer of kosher salt. Refrigerate, uncovered, for 15 minutes.

Place the potatoes in a medium saucepan and add enough cold water to cover by 1 inch. Bring to a boil, reduce the heat, and simmer until the potatoes are tender and easily pierced with a fork, about 10 to 15 minutes. Drain the potatoes, place in a large bowl, and mash with the milk and Old Bay.

Remove the cod from the refrigerator. Rinse the salt off and pat dry. Wipe any remaining salt from the baking dish, and return the fish to it. Sprinkle the cod with the parsley, drizzle with 1 tablespoon of olive oil, and top with the butter. Cover the dish with foil and bake the cod in the preheated oven until the fish is opaque and flakes easily with a fork, about 12 to 15 minutes. Lower the oven heat to 225°F.

Line a rimmed sheet pan with parchment paper or aluminum foil and line a plate with paper towels, and set both aside.

Remove the cod from the oven and use a fork to flake it into small pieces. Mix the cod, along with the oil and butter from the baking dish, into the potatoes. Add the eggs and ¼ cup of the cracker crumbs. Mix well to combine. Stir in more crumbs if the mixture is very wet. Shape the mixture into small patties about 2½ inches in diameter.

In a large, cast iron skillet, warm ¼-inch oil over medium-high heat. Working in batches and taking care not to crowd the pan, slip the coddies into the hot oil. Cook until the undersides are well browned, then flip and continue to fry until cooked through, about 4 to 5 minutes per side. Transfer the coddies to the plate lined with paper towels to drain, then place on the baking sheet and slide into the oven to keep warm. Add a little more oil to the pan, warm, and continue frying the coddies, adding oil between batches if needed. Serve hot.

STORAGE: *Leftover coddies will keep in an airtight container or wrapped in foil for 1 day in the refrigerator. Reheat in a 300°F oven before serving.*

How-To

If panfrying isn't your thing, you can oven-fry the coddies. Preheat the oven to 400°F. Generously oil the parchment-lined baking sheet. After shaping the patties, place them on the baking sheet, turn so both sides are oiled, and slide the sheet into the oven. Bake for 10 to 15 minutes, or until the undersides of the patties are browned. Flip and continue baking until cooked through, about 10 minutes more. Serve hot.

# Za'atar Pita Chips

MAKES 36 THICK OR 72 THIN CHIPS | PAREVE

*I remember how excited we got when pita and bagel chips hit the market. I think there was more to it than novelty and salt. There was just something really cool about see-ing breads we so associated with Israeli and Jewish culture turned into a mainstream snack. But fresh homemade chips are even better than the mass market versions, and best of all, you can customize them with your favorite spice blends; we're partial to za'atar—a blend of sumac, thyme, oregano, and sesame seeds.*

*Prep time: 5 minutes*
*Cook time: 5 minutes*

6 whole-wheat or plain pita breads
Extra-virgin olive oil
Za'atar
Kosher salt (optional)

Preheat the oven to 375°F. Place the pita breads in a stack on a cutting board. With a large, sharp knife, cut the pitas into 6 even wedges. If you prefer thicker chips, leave them as is. For thinner chips, carefully open each wedge and pull apart at the attached end, so you end up with 2 pita triangles from each wedge.

Line two large rimmed baking sheets with parchment paper. Spread the pita triangles in a single layer on the baking sheets. If you separated them into thin chips, lay them on the pan inside (textured side) up. If the pita triangles don't all fit, bake in batches.

Drizzle or brush both sides of the pitas with olive oil, then sprinkle the tops generously with za'atar and a couple of pinches of kosher salt, if using.

Bake in the preheated oven for about 5 to 7 min-utes, or until the chips begin to turn crisp and golden. For crunchier chips, leave them in lon-ger, but keep an eye on them—they can quickly go from toasty to burnt.

Remove the baking sheets from the oven, place them on racks, and sprinkle with extra za'atar if using. Serve warm or at room temperature. The chips will get crunchier as they cool.

**STORAGE**: *Once cool, place the chips in an air-tight container and store at room temperature for 2 to 3 days.*

> **Tip**
> Pair these chips with hummus, dips like the Moroccan-Spiced Carrot Dip or Muhammara, or soft cheese. Or crumble over salads or soup.

# Rye Soft Pretzels with Raspberry Mustard

MAKES 12 TO 16 PRETZELS | PAREVE

*Though my mother's parents made their home in Baltimore, most of their siblings and extended family remained in the City of Brotherly Love, and we visited fairly often. And as might be expected of a born and bred Philly girl, my grandmother had a deep love of hot soft pretzels, and exacting standards about what constituted good ones. I'm not quite sure what she'd make of my rye- and whole-wheat-enriched take on the snack, but I like to think she'd have enjoyed them. Maybe, with a little raspberry jam mixed in to sweeten the deal, she'd have forgiven my blasphemous use of Dijon instead of yellow mustard.*

*Prep time: 40 minutes*
*Rising time: 1 hour, 45 minutes*
*Cook time: 15 minutes*

### FOR THE PRETZELS

1½ cups warm water

1 tablespoon honey

1 package active dry yeast (2¼ teaspoons)

2 cups all-purpose flour

1 cup white whole-wheat flour

1 cup rye flour

2 teaspoons kosher salt or sea salt

### FOR THE BAKING SODA BATH

6 cups water

2 tablespoons baking soda

### FOR THE MUSTARD

¼ cup Dijon mustard

¼ cup raspberry preserves or seedless
   raspberry jam

**MAKE THE PRETZELS:** In a medium bowl, stir together the warm water and honey. Sprinkle the yeast over and allow to rest until it blooms and surface is foamy, about 5 to 10 minutes.

In a large bowl or stand mixer fitted with a dough hook, whisk together the flours and salt. Pour in the yeast mixture, and mix with a wooden spoon or the dough hook until the ingredients are well combined and the dough begins to pull into a ball. Knead by hand on a lightly floured surface for 8 to 10 minutes, or in the stand mixer for 5 minutes, until the dough is soft and smooth. Shape the dough into a ball.

Clean and dry the large mixing bowl, coat with a little oil, and return the dough to the bowl, turning to coat with the oil. Cover with plastic wrap or a tea towel, and allow to rise in a warm place until doubled in bulk, about 1 to 1½ hours.

Line two large rimmed baking sheets with parchment paper or silicone baking mats. Punch down the dough and transfer to a lightly floured work surface. Use a sharp knife to divide the dough into 12 to 16 equal pieces.

Take a piece of dough and roll it between your hands to form a rope, about 15 to 18 inches long. Lay the rope in a U shape, twist near the middle, and cross the "arms" to opposite sides at the bottom of the U to form a pretzel. Press the ends of the rope gently where they overlap the bottom of the pretzel to seal. Transfer the shaped pretzels to the baking sheets, cover with a tea towel, and allow to rest for 10 to 15 minutes. Preheat the oven to 450°F.

MAKE THE BAKING SODA BATH: In a large pot, stir together the water and baking soda. Bring to a boil. Working in batches, carefully add 2 to 3 pretzels to the baking soda bath, taking care not to crowd the pot. Cook for 30 seconds, turn the pretzels over, and cook 30 seconds more. Using a fine-mesh strainer or slotted spoon, fish the pretzels from the bath one at a time, transferring each back to the baking sheets. Continue with the remaining pretzels.

When all of the pretzels have had a boil in the baking soda bath, slide the pans into the preheated oven. Bake until golden brown, about 12 to 15 minutes, depending on the size. Transfer to a rack to cool slightly.

MAKE THE MUSTARD: While the pretzels are cooling, combine the mustard and raspberry preserves or jam in a small bowl. Mix well. Serve with the warm pretzels.

STORAGE: *The pretzels are tastiest the day they're made, but can be stored, well wrapped in foil, for 2 to 3 days at room temperature. Or, place the foil-wrapped pretzels in a freezer bag and freeze for up to 2 months. Reheat before serving in a 300°F oven.*

# Feta and Olives with Oregano

*My grandmother was such a devoted Hadassah leader that as soon as I was born, she ensured I had a life membership in the famed women's Zionist organization. (One of my earliest baby pictures features my membership pin tacked to my diaper.) She proudly served Israeli products whenever she could, and today, I do the same. And while this simple, delicious plate of feta and olives falls squarely in the category of a classic Greek mezze, it's a dish that's perfect for showcasing Israeli cheese, olives, and herbs.*

*Prep time: 5 minutes*

8 ounces good quality sheep's or cow's milk feta cheese

Dried oregano

Extra-virgin olive oil

Kalamata olives, or your favorite mix of black and green olives, drained

Slice the feta into ½-inch thick slabs. Arrange on a serving platter or individual plates.

Sprinkle each piece with a generous pinch of oregano, then drizzle with the olive oil.

Spoon 4 to 5 olives alongside each piece of feta. Serve immediately.

> Tip
>
> Serve warm pita, lavash, or flatbread with the feta.

# Nori and Smoked Salmon "Petits Fours"

SERVES 2 TO 4 | PAREVE

*My grandparents arrived home from Japan in the middle of the night, bearing treats for my mom and my aunt. What looked like beautiful petits fours glazed in green were actually seaweed-wrapped savories. Woken from a deep sleep, expecting to taste sweet but jolted by unfamiliar umami flavors, the girls were sorely disappointed. My mom swears the prank forever ruined sushi for her. (My aunt was not similarly afflicted.) Since the rest of the family loves Japanese food, I considered making maki or onigiri, but thought it would be more fun (and a little less fussy, assembly-wise) to give a nod to those "petits fours" with napoleon-style stacks inspired by a photo in Martha Stewart's Hors d'Oeuvres Handbook.*

*Prep time: 30 minutes*
*Cook time: 15 minutes*
*Chilling time: 4 hours, or overnight*

1½ cups sushi rice, rinsed until water runs clear

1¾ cups plus 2 tablespoons water

3 tablespoons unseasoned rice vinegar

1 tablespoon sugar

1 teaspoon salt

4 sheets toasted nori

½ English cucumber, peeled and very thinly sliced

1 mango, peeled, pitted, and very thinly sliced

1 avocado, peeled, pitted, and very thinly sliced

Pickled ginger, for serving

Wasabi, for serving

Tamari soy sauce, for serving

In a medium saucepan, combine the rice and water. Bring to a boil, cover, reduce the heat to low, and simmer for 15 minutes, or until the water is absorbed. Remove from the heat and allow the rice to rest, covered, for 5 minutes more.

In a small saucepan, combine the rice vinegar, sugar, and salt. Place over low heat and stir until the salt and sugar dissolve. Remove from the heat and pour the vinegar mixture over the rice, folding gently to combine.

Fill a small bowl with cool water and place it next to your work surface. Place a sheet of plastic wrap on the work surface. Lay a sheet of nori in the center of the plastic, shiny side down. Spoon ⅓ of the rice mixture onto the nori, and use the back of the spoon to spread the rice in an even layer to the edges of the nori sheet. Dip your fingers in the bowl of water and smooth the rice. Arrange the cucumber slices in a single layer over the rice. Top with another sheet of nori, placed shiny side down, and use your palms to gently compress the stack and smooth the nori.

Top with half of the remaining rice, smooth the surface with the back of the spoon and/or wet fingers, and top with the mango slices. Add another sheet of nori, shiny side down. Smooth and compress the stack again.

Top the nori with the rest of the rice, smooth it to the edges, and arrange the avocado over the rice. Finish the stack with a sheet of nori placed shiny side up. Top with another sheet of plastic wrap, smooth and compress the stack, and then wrap well in plastic. Place on a large plate and refrigerate for several hours or overnight.

To serve, take the stack from the refrigerator, remove the plastic wrap, and place on a cutting board. Use a very sharp knife to cut the stack along the score lines in the nori, wetting the knife between cuts to prevent sticking. Then cut through the resulting strips to create square stacks.

Transfer to a platter and serve with pickled ginger, wasabi, and tamari for dipping.

Simple Swap

For a non-vegetarian version, use thinly sliced smoked salmon for one of the layers.

# Oven Fries with Za'atar Aioli

SERVES 4 | PAREVE

*I got to know my now-husband in college, when we were both cast in the James Sherman play* The God of Isaac. *In one scene, Jewish journalist Isaac and his "shiksa goddess" wife spar over the meaning of various foods, ultimately deeming mustard Jewish, and mayo goyish. I laughed at the stereotype, because there was a certain truth to it. As a stand-alone condiment, my family never used mayonnaise. But I've developed an appreciation for it when it's seasoned zippily enough to give mustard a run for its money. I love the way za'atar and lemon cut mayonnaise's richness and lift its flavor. The aioli is a great complement to oven-roasted potatoes, which of course have near-universal appeal.*

*Prep time: 10 minutes*
*Cook time: 40 minutes*

### FOR THE OVEN FRIES

1½ to 2 pounds Russet potatoes, scrubbed
2 to 3 tablespoons extra-virgin olive oil
Pinch of kosher salt (optional)

### FOR THE ZA'ATAR AIOLI

⅓ cup mayonnaise
2 tablespoons za'atar
1 tablespoon freshly squeezed lemon juice

> **How-To**
>
> To approximate the texture of deep-fried potatoes, place the uncooked potato batons or wedges in a large bowl. Add enough cold water to cover by 1 inch, soak the potatoes for 30 minutes, drain, pat dry, and proceed with the recipe. The downside of this method is that it leaches a significant amount of potassium from the potatoes.

**MAKE THE OVEN FRIES:** Preheat the oven to 425°F. Line a large rimmed baking sheet with parchment paper. Cut the potatoes lengthwise into thick or thin wedges or batons, according to your shape and size preferences.

Spread the potatoes in a single layer on the baking sheet. Drizzle evenly with the oil, tossing with clean hands to thoroughly coat the potatoes in oil. Spread the potatoes out again, and slide the pan into the preheated oven. Roast until the undersides of the potatoes are golden, about 15 to 20 minutes, depending on size. Turn and roast for 10 to 20 minutes more, or until the fries are golden brown and crisp in spots.

**MAKE THE AIOLI:** While the potatoes are roasting, in a small bowl, mix together the mayonnaise and za'atar. Add the lemon juice and stir well.

When the potatoes are done, remove from the oven and season with kosher salt, if using. Transfer to a serving plate or bowl, and serve hot with the za'atar aioli for dipping.

# Charoset Three Ways

PAREVE

*I've always loved the moment in the Passover Seder when we taste the charoset—the fruit and nut mixture meant to symbolize the mortar used by the Israelite slaves in Egypt. My grandmother was always generous with the cinnamon and wine in the apple and walnut version passed down through her family, and she made enough to last into the week. Her recipe tastes like Pesach to me, and I look forward to enjoying it throughout the holiday.*

*My daughter, Riva, on the other hand doesn't like apples—or any fruit, really. Determined to create a recipe for this book, she excitedly announced she'd attempt a carrot charoset "for people like me." I wasn't sure whether my determined second grader had book material brewing—or even if it was possible to concoct charoset without fruit—but I promised we'd try. Her instincts were spot on, and we had a delicious charoset on our hands. More special still, I knew we were about to embark on a new Seder tradition, serving Riva's charoset alongside that of her namesake, my grandmother Ruth.*

*But it's not just the family's recipes I treasure. I'm fascinated by charoset, and the way its countless iterations reflect the scope and diversity of diaspora Jewry. Several years ago, we started a tradition to serve charoset from Jewish communities around the world alongside our own treasured family recipe. There may be no version simpler than the two-ingredient Iraqi charoset presented here, but the combination of nuts and date syrup is wonderful, and truly more than the sum of its parts.*

## Ruth's Apple and Walnut Charoset

*Makes about 3 cups*
*Prep time: 10 minutes*

4 apples peeled and coarsely grated (about 2 cups grated)

1 cup coarsely chopped walnuts

1 tablespoon cinnamon

2 to 4 tablespoons sweet red wine, such as Manischewitz or Kedem

In a large bowl, mix together the grated apples, walnuts, cinnamon, and 2 tablespoons of wine. Taste and add more cinnamon or wine if needed. *(CONTINUED)*

## Riva's Carrot and Almond Charoset

*Makes about 1½ cups*
*Prep time: 10 minutes*

6 large carrots, peeled
¾ cup raw almonds
1½ teaspoons cinnamon
1½ teaspoons ground ginger
3 tablespoons brown sugar
3 tablespoons honey
¼ to ⅓ cup dry red wine or grape juice

In a food processor fitted with an S blade, process the carrots until finely chopped. Add the almonds, cinnamon, ginger, brown sugar, and honey, and pulse several times, until the almonds are very finely chopped but the mixture still has texture.

Transfer to a large bowl. Add ¼ cup of wine or grape juice to the mixture. Mix well, taste, and add more wine or juice, 1 tablespoon at a time, mixing and tasting after each addition, until the desired flavor and texture are achieved.

## Iraqi Charoset

*Makes about 1 cup*
*Prep time: 5 minutes*

1 cup finely chopped raw walnuts
⅓ to 1 cup date syrup (silan)

In a medium bowl, place the walnuts. Drizzle date syrup over the nuts, stirring to coat. Adjust the quantity of nuts and date syrup to achieve a thick, mortar-like consistency.

STORAGE: *All three charoset recipes may be stored in airtight containers in the refrigerator for 4 to 5 days.*

### Did You Know?

Recent archeological finds indicate that there were apiaries in ancient Israel, but scholars agree that when the Torah calls Israel a "land of milk and honey," it is referring to date honey. Known as silan in Israel, and often called date syrup in the US, it's less intensely sweet than bee honey, but has a similar viscous, sticky texture. Making it involves simmering down dates, then extracting and reducing their juice until it reaches a syrup-like consistency. It's simpler to buy prepared date syrup, which you can find in Middle Eastern markets, some supermarkets, or online. For the best quality, look for one that doesn't contain added sugar.

Potato Latkes with Ras el Hanout and Lemon Zest (page 98)

# CHAPTER FOUR

# Salads and Vegetables

If there's one thing that has changed significantly since my grand-mothers' and great-grandmothers' time, it's the tremendous expansion of the produce aisle. Even mainstream supermarkets stock a far greater variety of fresh fruits and vegetables than our grandmothers had access to—to say nothing of the renaissance in farmers' markets and high-end grocery stores. For the bubbes of the world, who've long exhorted, "Eat your vegetables!" it must be vindicating to see nutrition science catch up with what they've always known about fostering health and making meals delicious.

# Two-Way Slaw

SERVES 4 TO 6 | PAREVE

*My grandmother made a great creamy coleslaw with poppy seeds, but she was also a fan of "health salad," the vinegary cousin to her mayo-dressed slaw, from the kosher deli. She often served them side by side—who doesn't like choice?—and since even a small head of cabbage yields an absurd amount of slaw once shredded, I've included both dressing options, so you can make some of each. Don't want to fuss with two types of slaw? Simply double the quantities for the dressing you prefer. You can eat the dressed slaws right away, but both get tastier after a few hours in the fridge.*

*Prep time: 10 minutes*

### FOR THE SLAW

1 medium head green cabbage (about
    2 pounds)
2 large carrots, peeled

### FOR THE CREAMY DRESSING

¼ cup mayonnaise
2 tablespoons white wine vinegar
    or rice vinegar
1 tablespoon sugar
½ teaspoon poppy seeds
¼ teaspoon kosher salt or sea salt

### FOR THE VINEGAR DRESSING

3 tablespoons apple cider vinegar
1 tablespoon neutral oil, such as
    grapeseed or canola
1 teaspoon sugar
½ teaspoon kosher salt or sea salt

**MAKE THE SLAW:** You can do this using a knife and box grater (option 1), or a food processor (option 2).

Option 1: Remove the tough outer leaves from the cabbage, core, and cut into large chunks. Using a large, sharp knife, slice the cabbage very thinly. Coarsely grate the carrot on a box grater.

Option 2: Fita food processor with a slicing disc. With the machine running, feed the cabbage chunks into the food processor to shred. Unplug the machine, change to the shredding disc, plug the processor back in, and shred the carrots.

Transfer the shredded cabbage and carrots in a large bowl. Toss together, then transfer half the cabbage mixture to a second bowl.

> **Tip**
>
> Use the food processor's shredding disk if you want a fine-cut slaw, akin to what you'd find in a Jewish deli. If you like longer cut cabbage in your slaw, use a slicing disk for the cabbage instead, then swap it for the shredding disc to grate the carrots.

**MAKE THE CREAMY DRESSING:** In a medium bowl, add the mayonnaise, vinegar, sugar, poppy seeds, and salt, and mix well. Toss with one bowl of the cabbage mixture, using clean hands or a large spoon, until well mixed. Cover and refrigerate until ready to serve.

**MAKE THE VINEGAR DRESSING:** In another medium bowl, add the apple cider vinegar, oil, sugar, and salt. Toss with the other bowl of the cabbage mixture, using clean hands or a large spoon, until well mixed. Cover and refrigerate until ready to serve.

**STORAGE:** *Slaw will keep, covered, in the refrigerator for 4 to 5 days.*

Tip

To add some crunch and color to the health salad, try mixing in chopped red bell peppers and/or tiny florets of blanched cauliflower.

# Purple Cabbage Slaw with Toasted Sesame Ginger Vinaigrette

SERVES 6 TO 8 | PAREVE

*This colorful slaw is a more savory nod to the "health salad" my grandmother often picked up at the kosher deli, and incorporates the Asian-inspired flavors she was so fond of. Thanks to the lack of perishable mayonnaise, it's a good choice for cookouts, picnics, and potlucks.*

*Prep time: 20 minutes*

## FOR THE SLAW

1 small to medium purple cabbage, outer leaves removed and discarded

1 red bell pepper, seeded and julienned

1 yellow bell pepper, seeded and julienned

2 carrots, peeled and julienned, or shredded

1 cup snow peas, trimmed, strings removed, and thinly sliced on the diagonal

2 scallions, white and green parts only, thinly sliced (optional)

¼ cup chopped fresh mint (optional)

## FOR THE VINAIGRETTE

½ cup rice vinegar or apple cider vinegar

¼ cup neutral oil, such as grapeseed or canola

2 tablespoons tamari soy sauce (reduced sodium is fine)

2 tablespoons brown sugar or pure maple syrup

1 tablespoon toasted sesame oil

1 tablespoon grated fresh ginger

**MAKE THE SLAW:** Quarter the cabbage and remove the tough core. Use a chef's knife or a food processor fitted with a slicing disc to cut the cabbage into thin shreds.

Put the cabbage in a large bowl. Add the peppers, carrots, and snow peas. Add the scallions and mint, if using. Toss to combine.

**MAKE THE VINAIGRETTE:** In a medium bowl, whisk the vinegar, oil, tamari, brown sugar or maple syrup, sesame oil, and ginger together until emulsified.

Pour the dressing over the cabbage mixture and toss to coat. Refrigerate, covered, until ready to serve.

# Arugula, Apple, and Date Salad with Goat Cheese and Pecans

SERVES 4 TO 6 | DAIRY OR PAREVE

*We're lucky on the salad front. In my grandmothers' day, supermarkets offered ice-berg lettuce and spinach. Now they sell mixed baby greens, herb salads, arugula, mache, and more, all triple washed for convenience. With so much choice, it's easy to take the bounty for granted. But a salad like this reminds me to be grateful that lettuce* ennui *is a thing of the past. Peppery arugula makes a delicious counterpoint to crisp, sweet-tart apple varieties, such as Sansa, Cameo, Mutsu, or Pink Lady. The goat cheese is optional, but highly recommended—its creamy tang is a fabulous accent to the dates and pecans.*

*Prep time: 15 minutes*

### FOR THE SALAD

1 (5-ounce) package baby arugula, rinsed and spun dry

2 apples, cored and thinly sliced

6 to 8 Medjool dates, pitted and quartered lengthwise

2½ ounces plain or herbed goat cheese, crumbled (optional)

⅓ cup raw or dry-roasted pecan halves or pieces

### FOR THE VINAIGRETTE

¼ cup extra-virgin olive oil

2 tablespoons balsamic vinegar

1 tablespoon pure maple syrup, preferably dark

2 garlic cloves, finely chopped

**MAKE THE SALAD:** Place the arugula in a large bowl. Add the apple slices and toss gently to combine. Top with the dates, goat cheese if using, and pecans.

**MAKE THE VINAIGRETTE:** In a medium bowl, whisk together the olive oil, balsamic vinegar, maple syrup, and garlic. Transfer the dressing to a cruet or serving bowl and serve alongside the salad.

# Roasted Beet Salad with Ginger and Garlic Vinaigrette

SERVES 4 | PAREVE

*My grandmother made a valiant effort to turn me on to beets. She sang their praises as fortifiers of the blood, pointed out their gorgeous fuchsia hue, and offered them up sliced and pickled, or puréed into borscht. She got nowhere with me, a little kid suspicious of anything pickled that wasn't a cucumber. I didn't take to beets' mineral sweetness and unusual texture until I was well into my twenties, when I first tasted them from a New York City greenmarket, roasted and served in a salad like this one.*

**Prep time: 15 minutes**
**Cook time: 1 hour**

2 medium red beets, cleaned and trimmed of their greens

2 medium golden beets, cleaned and trimmed of their greens

¼ cup extra-virgin olive oil, plus extra for the beets

¼ cup unseasoned rice vinegar or white wine vinegar

1- to 1½-inch piece fresh ginger, peeled and finely grated

2 large garlic cloves, finely chopped

Sea salt

Freshly ground black pepper

5 ounces mixed baby greens, rinsed and spun dry

### Note

If you can't find golden beets, more reds are fine. And if you're lucky enough to find beets with their greens attached, save them—the leaves and tender stems are delicious sautéed in olive oil and garlic.

Preheat the oven to 400°F. Rub the skin of each beet with a little olive oil. Wrap the red beets loosely in a piece of foil and wrap the golden beets loosely in another piece of foil. (If you wrap them together, the colors will bleed.)

Lay the wrapped beets on a rimmed baking sheet and place in the preheated oven. Roast for 45 to 60 minutes, or until tender. The larger the beets, the longer they'll take to roast. Remove the sheet from the oven and set it aside until the beets are cool enough to handle. Peel the beets, and cut them into bite-size pieces.

In a medium bowl, make the vinaigrette by whisking together the olive oil and vinegar. Add the ginger and garlic and whisk to emulsify. Season with salt and pepper.

Place the baby greens in a large bowl and top with the beets. Drizzle about half the vinaigrette over the beets and greens, then toss to coat. Serve immediately with the remaining dressing on the side.

# Grapefruit, Avocado, and Sardine Salad with Za'atar Croutons

SERVES 4 TO 6 | PAREVE

*My grandfather loved sardines, and long before nutritionists were touting the benefits of omega-3 fatty acids, my grandmother was a big advocate of fish as "brain food." As a kid, I didn't like the look of the little oil-slicked fish crammed into their tin. And the mere mention of brains in relation to food turned me off. When I finally tasted sardines, they were fresh, served whole straight off the grill. It wasn't hard to make the leap to canned sardines; now I consider them a pantry staple. Though we usually just pop open a can for a quick snack, sometimes it's nice to dress up the humble little fish. In this composed salad, their briny flavor is a great counterpoint to tart, juicy grapefruit, mellow avocado, and crunchy za'atar croutons.*

*Prep time: 15 minutes*
*Cook time: 15 minutes*

### FOR THE CROUTONS

8 ounces challah, cut into ¾-inch cubes

2 tablespoons extra-virgin olive oil

2 tablespoons za'atar

¼ teaspoon kosher salt or sea salt

### FOR THE SALAD

2 ruby red grapefruits

2 ripe avocados, halved, pitted, and sliced lengthwise

2 cans sardines, skinless, boneless, and packed in olive oil

### FOR THE VINAIGRETTE

⅓ cup extra-virgin olive oil

2 tablespoons balsamic vinegar

1 teaspoon Dijon mustard

1 teaspoon honey (optional)

1 large garlic clove, finely chopped

**MAKE THE CROUTONS:** Preheat the oven to 350°F. Place the challah cubes on a rimmed baking sheet. Drizzle them with the olive oil, and sprinkle with the za'atar and salt. Toss to coat. Bake for 10 to 15 minutes (or to desired crispness), turning once or twice while cooking to toast evenly. Set aside to cool.

**MAKE THE SALAD:** Using a sharp knife, prepare the grapefruit by trimming the ends off of each one, so the fruit is exposed and no white pith remains. Set one of the flat ends on a cutting board, and following the shape of fruit, use the knife to remove all of the skin and pith. Working over a small bowl to catch the juice, remove the segments by carefully slicing between the fruit and the thin white membranes that hold it in place. Place the segments in the bowl as you work. (Squeeze any leftover juice from the membranes when you're done removing the segments—you won't need it for the recipe, but you can drink it!) *(CONTINUED)*

On a platter or individual serving plates, arrange the grapefruit segments and avocado slices, alternating between each. Mound some of the croutons in the center, then lay the sardines against them to build up the center of the salad, while showing off the fruit underneath.

MAKE THE VINAIGRETTE: In a cruet or small bowl, combine the oil, vinegar, mustard, honey (if using), and garlic. Shake or whisk to combine. Drizzle over the salad, serving any extra on the side.

# Spinach Salad with Roasted Mushrooms and Quick-Pickled Red Onions

SERVES 8 TO 10 | DAIRY

*There are recipes that enjoy a certain fame among friends—ones they clamor for whenever they're invited to dinner. My grandmother's spinach salad was the sort that inspired inquiries. It was simple, really—just spinach topped with sliced raw onions and mushrooms, chopped eggs, and faux bacon bits—but the creamy, savory dressing turned it into something special. I've updated the recipe by roasting the mushrooms and treating the red onions to a quick pickle to mellow their sharpness. My grandmother used "salad oil," because that's what was available in her time, but I prefer the flavor (and healthier profile) of olive oil, and think she would have embraced the switch.*

*Prep time: 15 minutes*
*Cook time: 30 minutes*

### FOR THE DRESSING

½ cup extra-virgin olive oil

2 tablespoons plus 1½ teaspoons red wine vinegar

2 tablespoons sour cream

1 tablespoon sugar

1 tablespoon chopped parsley

2 garlic cloves, finely chopped

¾ teaspoon sea salt or kosher salt

¼ teaspoon dry mustard

### FOR ONIONS

1 red onion, very thinly sliced

⅓ cup red wine vinegar

1 teaspoon sugar

½ teaspoon kosher salt or sea salt

### FOR THE SALAD

1 pound cremini, shiitake, portobello, or other favorite mushrooms (or a mix)

2 tablespoons extra-virgin olive oil

2 tablespoons chopped fresh parsley, chives, or garlic

1 pound baby spinach, rinsed and spun dry

4 hardboiled eggs, peeled and quartered

Vegetarian bacon strips, cooked according to package directions (optional)

*(CONTINUED)*

**MAKE THE DRESSING:** In a medium bowl, whisk together the olive oil, vinegar, sour cream, sugar, parsley, garlic, salt, and mustard. Cover and refrigerate until ready to use, whisking again just before serving.

**PICKLE THE ONIONS:** Place the onions in a nonreactive bowl. In another small bowl, whisk together the vinegar, sugar, and salt until mostly dissolved. Pour the mixture over the onions, toss to coat, and set aside for at least 30 minutes. (If you're pickling the onions further in advance, cover and refrigerate until ready to use.)

**MAKE THE SALAD:** Preheat the oven to 425°F. Line a rimmed baking sheet with parchment paper. Clean and trim the mushrooms, remove any woody stems, and halve or quarter them if they're large. Place the mushrooms in a single layer in a roasting pan or rimmed baking sheet.

Drizzle with the olive oil, sprinkle with the herbs, and toss to coat. Roast in the preheated oven for 25 to 30 minutes, stirring once or twice during cooking, until the mushrooms are caramelized in spots. Set aside.

To serve, place the baby spinach in a large bowl. Add the roasted mushrooms and pickled onions (without their pickling liquid) and toss to coat. Arrange the egg quarters around the salad. Sprinkle with crumbled faux bacon, if using. Serve the salad with the dressing on the side.

How-To

Need help making perfect hardboiled eggs? Check out the method in Deviled Eggs with Chives and Smoked Paprika (page 57).

# Asparagus with Smoky Pepper Vinaigrette

SERVES 4 | PAREVE

*We may take its year-round supermarket presence for granted now, but fresh aspar-agus wasn't always so easy to find. My grandmother took what she could get, and that meant jars of pickled asparagus. Pea-green and slick thanks to its acidic marinade, it didn't appeal to my young palate. But her assurances that the fresh veggie was very different from its jarred counterpart stuck with me. When, as a college student, I found the stalks standing at attention in the farmers' market, I grabbed a bunch, and discovered that I shared my grandmother's passion for asparagus. I've since made it countless times and in many ways. But in tribute to my grandmother, I couldn't think of a better preparation than to dress the vibrant steamed stalks with a piquant vin-aigrette, as a wink and nod to those jars of pickled asparagus.*

*Prep time: 5 minutes*
*Cook time: 10 minutes*

1 tablespoon extra-virgin olive oil

2 garlic cloves, minced

1 red bell pepper, cored, seeded, and cut into
   ¼-inch dice

1 yellow or orange bell pepper, cored, seeded,
   and cut into ¼-inch dice

1 tablespoon balsamic vinegar

1 tablespoon date syrup or honey

Smoked paprika

Sea salt or kosher salt

1 bunch asparagus, woody ends trimmed

### Tip

To serve this dish chilled, refrigerate the cooked asparagus and vinaigrette separately. Before serving, remove the vinaigrette from the refrigerator and let it come to room temperature. Stir to emulsify, then pour over the chilled asparagus.

First, make the vinaigrette. In a large skillet set over medium-high heat, warm the oil. Add the garlic and sauté for 30 seconds. Add the peppers and sauté 3 to 5 minutes more, or until the peppers begin to soften. Stir in the vinegar and date syrup or honey. Cook for 1 to 2 minutes, stirring frequently, until slightly reduced. Season to taste with smoked paprika and a pinch of salt. Remove from the heat and set aside.

Next, make the asparagus. Add ½-inch of water to a chef's pan or large, deep skillet. Place over high heat and bring to a boil. Add the asparagus spears and cook, turning once or twice, until the asparagus is bright green and crisp-tender, about 2 to 5 minutes, depending on the thickness of the stalks. Drain and transfer the asparagus to a platter.

Spoon the warm vinaigrette over the asparagus, leaving the tips and ends exposed. Serve warm or at room temperature.

# Romanesco with Golden Raisins and Toasted Almonds

SERVES 4 TO 6 | PAREVE

*A longtime schoolteacher, my grandmother was fascinated by theoretical math, though she always copped to "cheating" on simple arithmetic by counting on her knuckles. Unless she encountered it while visiting Italy, I don't think she ever saw Romanesco, a gorgeous relative of cauliflower and broccoli with striking fractal spirals, but I'm sure she'd have found it entrancing. If you can't find it at your farmers' market, white, orange, or purple cauliflower (or a mix) are good substitutes in this recipe. The dish is lovely as is, but drizzles of nutty tahini and date syrup (silan) play up the savory and sweet interplay of the Romanesco, almonds, and raisins.*

*Prep time: 10 minutes*
*Cook time: 15 to 25 minutes*

1 large head Romanesco, broken into small florets

2 tablespoons extra-virgin olive oil

¼ cup sliced raw almonds

¼ cup golden raisins

Kosher salt or flaky sea salt

Freshly ground black pepper

Tahini (optional)

Date syrup (optional)

Preheat the oven to 425°F. Place the Romanesco florets in a single layer on a rimmed baking sheet and drizzle with the olive oil. Toss to coat. Place in the oven and roast, stirring once or twice. Roast for about 15 minutes for crisp-tender vegetables, or 20 to 25 minutes for softer, more caramelized florets.

While the Romanesco is roasting, toast the almonds. Place them in a dry, heavy skillet set over medium heat and stir or gently shake the pan often, just until the almonds are golden and have a toasty aroma, about 2 minutes. Remove from the heat and set aside.

Transfer the Romanesco to a serving dish. Toss it with the almonds and raisins. Season with a pinch kosher salt and a few grinds pepper. Drizzle with tahini and/or date syrup if using. Serve hot.

**STORAGE:** *Leftover Romanesco will keep, covered, in the refrigerator for 1 to 2 days.*

# Butternut Purée with Roasted Garlic and Ginger

SERVES 4 TO 6 | PAREVE

*Like many grandmothers of a certain generation, mine served up a marshmallow-topped, pineapple-flecked sweet potato casserole for Thanksgiving and Chanukah. Like most kids, I loved the toasty marshmallow topping best. This butternut purée is loosely inspired by the vibrant sweet potato mash beneath that sugary cloak. Roasted garlic adds a savory element to balance the sweetness of the squash, while dark maple syrup lends a sweet touch with nuance.*

*Prep time: 10 minutes*
*Cook time: 40 minutes*

1 large butternut squash (about 4 pounds)

1 head garlic

Extra-virgin olive oil (for the baking dish and garlic)

1 tablespoon virgin coconut oil or olive oil

1 (1-inch) piece fresh ginger, peeled and finely grated (about 1 tablespoon)

1 tablespoon pure maple syrup (preferably dark)

Sea salt or kosher salt (optional)

Preheat the oven to 425°F. Oil a baking dish large enough to hold the squash halves. Trim the stem from the squash, halve lengthwise, and scoop out the seeds. Place the squash halves face down in the prepared baking dish.

Keeping the head intact, peel away the papery outer layers from the garlic. Trim off the pointy end so the tops of the garlic cloves are visible. Place the head on a square of foil, drizzle the exposed cloves with olive oil, and wrap the head of garlic in the foil. Place the foil package in the baking dish with the squash. Roast in the preheated oven for 40 minutes, or until the squash is tender.

Remove the baking dish from the oven. Reduce the heat to 350°F. When the squash is cool enough to handle, scoop the flesh into a bowl. Squeeze the roasted garlic cloves from their skins and add to the squash. Stir with a fork or whisk to mash.

Stir in the coconut or olive oil, ginger, and maple syrup. Season with a pinch of salt, if using. Using an immersion blender or food processor, purée the squash mixture until smooth.

Transfer the squash to a baking dish. Return to the oven for 10 to 15 minutes, or until heated through.

**STORAGE:** *Leftover squash will keep, covered, in the refrigerator for 3 to 4 days.*

# Maple Dijon–Glazed Brussels Sprouts

SERVES 4 TO 6 | DAIRY OR PAREVE

*Brussels sprouts have enjoyed a renaissance in recent years, as folks have discovered that the much-maligned veggie can be quite delicious when prepared respectfully. The growing availability of fresh sprouts led cooks to discover that the adorable little cabbages—formerly subjected to freezing and boiling—had unknown charm to spare. Note that some consider fresh Brussels sprouts problematic from a kosher point of view, because of concerns over the difficulty of checking for bug infestation. Some authorities allow the use of shredded fresh Brussels sprouts, which can be substituted in the recipe below (cooking time will be shorter). Others permit the use of frozen sprouts if they have a hechsher (kosher certification).*

*Prep time: 10 minutes*
*Cook time: 10 minutes*

2 tablespoons Dijon mustard

2 tablespoons pure maple syrup (preferably dark)

2 tablespoons freshly squeezed lemon juice

4 teaspoons extra-virgin olive oil

4 teaspoons unsalted butter (or more oil)

1½ pounds Brussels sprouts, tough outer leaves removed, trimmed, and quartered

Freshly ground black pepper

### How-To

If you have kashrut concerns about fresh Brussels sprouts, you can use frozen (it's fine to leave them whole). Preheat the oven to 425°F. Place the sprouts in a single layer in a roasting pan. Drizzle with olive oil, dot with butter (if using), and roast for 20 minutes, or until the sprouts heat through and turn tender and caramelized. Add the mustard-maple mixture, toss to coat, and roast, stirring once or twice, about 10 minutes more.

In a small bowl, whisk together the Dijon mustard, maple syrup, and lemon juice. Set aside.

In a chef's pan or large, deep skillet set over medium-high heat, warm the oil and butter, stirring with a spatula to combine. When the butter melts and foams, stir in the Brussels sprouts. Sauté until the Brussels sprouts are bright green and tender, about 5 to 7 minutes.

Pour the mustard-maple mixture over the Brussels sprouts. Sauté for 1 to 2 minutes, or until the Brussels sprouts are glazed and the sauce is warmed through. Season to taste with black pepper.

# Colcannon with Kale

SERVES 4 | DAIRY OR PAREVE

*My grandmother Ruth's maiden name was Morrison, and her father was of Irish extraction. Before she was born, her family moved several times, and she had siblings born throughout the British Isles. She was the baby of the family and the first child born in the United States, but she was especially proud of her combination of Russian and Irish roots. Her mashed potatoes were well loved, so my thoughts turn to her when I make colcannon. Though many make it with cabbage, kale is a traditional addition, too.*

**Prep time: 10 minutes**
**Cook time: 25 minutes**

2 large russet potatoes, peeled and cut into 1-inch pieces (about 1½ pounds)

2 tablespoons unsalted butter or extra virgin olive oil, divided

1 large bunch kale, rinsed, tough center stems removed, leaves chopped

½ cup milk or soy milk

¼ to ½ teaspoon nutmeg

Sea salt (optional)

Place the potatoes in a large saucepan with enough cold water to cover by 1 inch. Bring to a boil, then reduce the heat and simmer until the potatoes are easily pierced with a fork, about 15 to 20 minutes.

While the potatoes cook, prepare the kale. In a chef's pan or large, deep skillet set over medium-high heat, melt 1 tablespoon of butter or oil. Add the kale and sauté until it turns bright green and wilts, about 3 to 5 minutes. Remove from the heat and set aside.

When the potatoes are tender, remove from the heat and drain. Return them to the saucepan, and mash with a fork or wire whisk. Add the other tablespoon of butter or oil, the milk or soy milk, and ¼ teaspoon of nutmeg. Mash until the potatoes reach your preferred consistency.

Stir in the kale, mixing well so it is evenly incorporated. Taste and adjust the seasoning, adding more nutmeg and/or sea salt if using. Transfer to a serving dish.

# Potato Latkes with Ras el Hanout and Lemon Zest

SERVES 4 TO 6 | PAREVE

*Conventional wisdom says latkes should be made with russet potatoes. And many will say the only acceptable oil is something with a high smoke point, like peanut—which my grandmother used—or canola. In grad school, we often heard that extra-virgin olive oil should only be used cold for finishing dishes. But those assertions just don't hold water, either scientifically or anthropologically. None other than the estimable Marcella Hazan called the arguments against frying with extra-virgin olive oil a "canard." The miracle of Chanukah is directly tied to olive oil, so I've never seen the point in frying latkes in anything else. And it's definitely the best complement to the Mediterranean flavors in these latkes.*

*Prep time: 25 minutes*
*Cook time: 25 minutes*

### FOR THE RAS EL HANOUT

2 teaspoons ground ginger

2 teaspoons ground coriander

1½ teaspoons ground cumin

1½ teaspoons ground cardamom

1½ teaspoons freshly ground black pepper

1¼ teaspoons nutmeg

1 teaspoon turmeric

1 teaspoon allspice

1 teaspoon cinnamon

1 teaspoon hot Spanish paprika

½ teaspoon cayenne pepper

Generous pinch saffron threads

### FOR THE LATKES

1 pound Yukon gold potatoes, peeled

1 medium onion, peeled

1 large egg, lightly beaten

¼ cup all-purpose flour

1 tablespoon ras el hanout

1 teaspoon salt

Zest of 1 lemon

Olive oil for frying

### FOR SERVING

Applesauce

Sour cream

### Did You Know?

There's no set recipe for ras el hanout, a complexly nuanced spice blend that can contain 30 to 40 spices. The name translates as "top of the shop," and is a clue to its importance to Moroccan cuisine, and the quality of spices that go in it. My version contains "only" a dozen, but it's easy to make, since it uses ground spices that don't require toasting.

**MAKE THE RAS EL HANOUT:** In a medium bowl, whisk together the ginger, coriander, cumin, cardamom, black pepper, nutmeg, turmeric, allspice, cinnamon, paprika, and cayenne. Crush the saffron, add to the spice mixture, and whisk again. Spoon the ras el hanout into a spice jar or airtight container.

**MAKE THE LATKES:** Preheat the oven to 200°F. Line a rimmed baking sheet with parchment paper or foil. Line a plate with paper towels for draining the fried latkes and set aside.

Use a box grater or a food processor fitted with a grating disk to grate the potatoes. Place a large colander in a bowl. Put the grated potatoes into the colander and press down with your hands or the back of a spoon to extract some of the liquid. Leave the potatoes to drain.

Grate the onion with the grater or food processor. Add the onion to the colander and press the vegetables, extracting as much liquid as possible.

Lift the colander out of the bowl and set aside. Take the bowl of liquid to the sink. Slowly pour off the liquid, but try to save as much of the white potato starch that has accumulated in the bottom of the bowl as you can.

To the bowl with the potato starch, add the drained potatoes, onions, and egg. Mix well. Sprinkle the flour evenly over the potato

mixture, and stir to incorporate. Add the ras el hanout, salt, and lemon zest. Mix just until the spices are evenly distributed.

In a large, heavy skillet (cast iron is ideal) set over medium-high heat, add ¼-inch of oil. When the oil is hot and shimmery but not smoking, add the latke batter in heaping tablespoons, taking care not to crowd the pan. Flatten slightly and fry for about 2 to 3 minutes per side, or until golden. (Most skillets will hold about 4 latkes; you can cook in 2 skillets simultaneously if you'd like to finish frying more quickly.)

As the latkes finish frying, transfer them to a plate lined with paper towels to drain. Then place on the baking sheet and transfer to the oven to keep them warm while you fry the remaining latkes in batches. If the oil level dwindles, add more to the pan between batches and heat it back to frying temperature before proceeding.

When all of the latkes are cooked, serve immediately with applesauce and/or sour cream.

**STORAGE:** *Though they taste best fresh, leftover latkes can be frozen, well wrapped with parchment or wax paper between them. Reheat in a 375°F oven until hot and crisp. If you start with fresh spices, ras el hanout can be stored for up to 6 months in a cool, dark place.*

Farro Salad with Lemony White Beans, Roasted Red Peppers, and Cauliflower (page 115)

# CHAPTER FIVE

# Grains

On my grandmother's table, grains were quiet supporting players. Rice, lokshen (egg noodles), or kasha varnishkes (buckwheat groats with bow tie noodles and onions) served as much to sop up sauces and give the palate a rest from more elaborately flavored dishes as to nourish. They were comforting, but incredibly simple. Today, our options have expanded tremendously, with ancient grains and international offerings available in most supermarkets. Accented with beans, vegetables, herbs, or fruit, these grains are exciting enough to take center stage.

# Basmati Rice with Sweet Carrot and Orange

SERVES 4 | PAREVE

*Many of my grandmother's recipes include the simple directive "serve with rice." Where she would have used plain white rice, this dish, infused with gently sweetened carrot and orange zest, would make a lovely alternative. The flavors are loosely inspired by Shirin Polo—a far more elaborate Persian dish popular for festive occasions like weddings—but this simple version can work beautifully with a wide range of cuisines.*

*Prep time: 5 minutes*
*Cook time: 20 minutes*

1½ cups basmati rice
2¾ cups water
Pinch kosher salt or sea salt
1 tablespoon extra-virgin olive oil
1 carrot, peeled and finely grated
Zest of 1 orange, finely grated
1 tablespoon honey

### Simple Swap

For a whole-grain version, use brown basmati rice instead of white, and adjust the cooking time and water quantity accordingly per the package directions— the rice will take about 50 minutes, rather than 15.

Place the rice in a fine-mesh strainer and rinse well under cold running water. Drain and transfer to a medium saucepan. Add the water and salt. Bring to a boil, reduce the heat, and simmer, covered, until the water is absorbed and the rice is tender, about 15 minutes. Remove from the heat and allow the rice to rest, covered, while you make the carrots.

In a small skillet set over medium heat, warm the oil. Add the carrot and sauté for 2 to 3 minutes. Add the orange zest and honey. Sauté until the mixture is fragrant and the honey melts and coats the carrots and orange zest, about 1 to 2 minutes.

Pour the carrot mixture over the hot rice, using a silicone spatula to scrape the syrup from the skillet. Fold the mixture into the rice until the carrots and zest are distributed throughout. Serve hot.

# Ema's Cold Rice Salad

SERVES 6 TO 8 | PAREVE

*Sometimes recipes get passed from kid to parent, which is what happened here. Ema (my mother) made this cold rice salad, her mom liked it, and it ended up on everyone's table. Back in the 1980s they'd opt for Minute Rice and bottled Italian dressing, but since the recipe is so quick and easy to prepare from scratch, I've skipped the shortcuts.*

*Prep time: 15 minutes*
*Cook time: 30 minutes*

### FOR THE RICE

1½ cups basmati or jasmine rice
2¼ cups water

### FOR THE VINAIGRETTE

¼ cup red wine vinegar
Freshly squeezed juice of ½ lemon
1 teaspoon honey or sugar
1 garlic clove, finely chopped
1 teaspoon dried oregano
½ teaspoon dried basil
⅓ cup extra-virgin olive oil

### FOR THE VEGETABLES

1 large orange bell pepper, seeded
    and chopped
1 large yellow bell pepper, seeded
    and chopped
1 large seedless cucumber (such as English
    or hothouse), peeled and chopped
1 medium yellow or red onion, peeled
    and chopped
2 large tomatoes, peeled, seeded,
    and chopped

**MAKE THE RICE:** Place the rice in a fine-mesh strainer and rinse well under cold running water. Drain and transfer to a medium saucepan. Add the water and bring to a boil over high heat. Reduce the heat to low, cover, and simmer for 15 to 20 minutes, or until the water is absorbed and the rice is tender. Remove from the heat and let the rice stand, covered, while you make the vinaigrette.

**MAKE THE VINAIGRETTE:** In a medium bowl, whisk together the red wine vinegar, lemon juice, honey or sugar, garlic, oregano, and basil. Slowly add the olive oil while whisking, until emulsified.

Spread the rice evenly in a 9-by-13-by-2-inch or similar size casserole dish, and smooth the top gently with a spatula. Whisk the vinaigrette again and drizzle half evenly over the rice.

*(CONTINUED)*

MAKE THE VEGETABLES: Arrange half the orange peppers on top of the rice in a lengthwise stripe running down one side of the dish. Repeat on the other side. Make stripes with the yellow pepper alongside the orange. Repeat with the cucumber, then onions, working your way toward the middle of the dish. Make a single stripe with the tomatoes down the center. The vegetables should cover the rice almost completely.

Whisk the remaining vinaigrette once more, and pour evenly over the vegetables. Cover and refrigerate until ready to serve.

STORAGE: *Leftover salad will keep, covered, in the refrigerator for 2 to 3 days.*

# Forbidden Rice Salad with Mango and Ginger Vinaigrette

SERVES 6 TO 8 | PAREVE

*My grandmother's interest in China went far deeper than a stereotypical Jewish interest in the food. Apparently, the family's migrations had taken us to China at one point, and an uncle was born there. Much to her consternation, the Bamboo Curtain thwarted my grandmother's desire to ever visit the country, but she had a local Chinese artisan make much of her furniture. Ladies carved from jade decorated the hand-painted surfaces, and she knew all of the folk tales they depicted. Had forbidden rice been available while she was alive, I have no doubt she would have relished sharing the story that the gorgeously hued grains were once reserved exclusively for the emperor. Maybe she, too, would have served it in a fresh take on Ema's Cold Rice Salad.*

*Prep time: 15 minutes*
*Cook time: 35 minutes*

### FOR THE RICE

2 ¾ cups water
1 ½ cups forbidden (black) rice

### FOR THE DRESSING

½ cup unseasoned rice vinegar
⅓ cup neutral oil, such as grapeseed or canola
2 tablespoons tamari soy sauce
1 ½ tablespoons pure maple syrup
1 ½ teaspoons toasted sesame oil
1 teaspoon finely grated fresh ginger

### FOR THE VEGETABLES

1 large red bell pepper, seeded and chopped
1 large yellow bell pepper, seeded and chopped
1 large seedless cucumber (such as English or hothouse), peeled and chopped
1 medium Vidalia onion, peeled and chopped
1 mango, peeled, seeded, and chopped

**MAKE THE RICE:** Combine the water and rice in a medium saucepan, and bring to a boil over high heat. Reduce the heat to low, cover, and simmer for 30 to 35 minutes, or until the water is absorbed and the rice is tender. Remove from the heat and let the rice stand, covered, while you make the vinaigrette.

**MAKE THE DRESSING:** In a medium bowl, whisk together the rice vinegar, oil, tamari, maple syrup, sesame oil, and ginger.

Spread the rice evenly in a 9-by-13-by-2-inch casserole dish, and smooth the top gently with a spatula. Whisk the vinaigrette again and pour half evenly over the rice. *(CONTINUED)*

MAKE THE VEGETABLES: Arrange half the red peppers on top of the rice in a lengthwise stripe running down one side of the dish. Repeat on the other side. Make stripes with the yellow peppers alongside the red. Repeat with the cucumber, then onion, working your way toward the middle of the dish. Make a single stripe with the mango down the center. The vegetables and mango should be covering the rice almost completely.

Whisk the remaining vinaigrette once more, and pour evenly over the vegetables. Cover and refrigerate until ready to serve.

STORAGE: *Leftover salad will keep, covered, in the refrigerator for 2 to 3 days.*

Tip

To add visual and textural interest to the salad, try cutting the cucumbers as food stylist Laurie Knoop did in the photo on the facing page—leave the peels on the cucumber, quarter it lengthwise, then thinly slice it crosswise. You'll end up with almost triangular slices.

# Barley and Roasted Vegetable Salad

SERVES 4 TO 6 | PAREVE

*Barley, like lima beans, was one of the things I loved to find in vegetable soup as a kid. It sometimes made an appearance in my grandmother's mushroom barley soup, but I never saw it outside of a soup bowl. Now it's one of my go-tos for pilafs and grain salads. Though pearled barley isn't technically a whole grain, it's still far more fiber- and nutrient-rich than most polished grains, and cooks much more quickly than hulled barley (hull-less varieties are now being grown, and would work here too). Barley is also one the Seven Species of Israel (see the tip), so I like to use this salad on my Sukkot and Shavuot menus.*

*Prep time: 15 minutes*
*Cook time: 25 minutes*

FOR THE SALAD

1 pint grape or cherry tomatoes, halved
    lengthwise if large

1 bunch asparagus, tough ends snapped,
    cut into ½-inch pieces, tips left whole

1 cup fresh or frozen corn kernels

1 orange bell pepper

Extra-virgin olive oil

1½ cups pearled or hull-less barley

3 cups water

FOR THE DRESSING

⅓ cup freshly squeezed lemon juice

¼ cup extra-virgin olive oil

¼ teaspoon sea salt or kosher salt

2 tablespoons finely chopped fresh basil,
    plus extra for garnish

MAKE THE SALAD: Preheat the oven to 425°F. Spread the tomatoes, cut side up (if halved), in a single layer on a small rimmed baking sheet or in a baking dish. Place the asparagus pieces in a single layer in another baking dish. Do the same with the corn kernels. Place the whole pepper in a small baking dish. (For easier cleanup, line the baking pans with foil.) Drizzle the tomatoes, asparagus, and corn with a little olive oil and toss to coat. Rub a bit of oil all over the pepper.

Place the dishes in the preheated oven and roast the vegetables, stirring the tomatoes, asparagus, and corn, and turning the pepper once or twice, until the tomatoes start to burst and release their juices, the asparagus and corn begin to caramelize, and pepper skin begins to char, about 10 to 12 minutes for the asparagus, and 20 to 25 minutes for the other vegetables. Keep an eye on the vegetables and remove them from the oven as they reach your preferred level of doneness. Set aside to cool slightly. When the pepper is cool enough to touch, peel, core, and seed it, then chop it into ¼-inch pieces.

While the vegetables roast, rinse the barley in a fine-mesh strainer under cool running water until the water runs clear. In a medium saucepan, combine the barley and 3 cups of water. Bring to a boil, reduce the heat to low, and simmer, partially covered, until the barley is tender but al dente, about 15 to 20 minutes. Drain and rinse the barley, and transfer to a large bowl.

Stir the tomatoes, along with any pan juices, into the barley. Add the asparagus, corn, and peppers, and toss well.

MAKE THE DRESSING: In a small bowl, whisk together the lemon juice, olive oil, and salt. Pour over the salad and mix well. Stir in 2 tablespoons of chopped basil. Serve warm or at room temperature, garnished with additional basil.

STORAGE: *Leftover salad will keep, covered, in the refrigerator for 3 to 4 days.*

Did You Know?

The Seven Species of Israel, or Shivat Haminim, have been important fixtures in Israeli food and religious observance since antiquity. In the book of Devarim (Deuteronomy), the Torah calls Israel "a land of wheat, and barley, and vines, and fig trees, and pomegranates; a land of olive oil and honey." The first fruits of these crops were brought to the Beit HaMikdash (Holy Temple) in Jerusalem and the products of some, like wheat flour, wine, and olive oil, were regularly used in the temple service. Today, it's a tradition to incorporate the Seven Species into menus for the major harvest holidays, as well festivals that celebrate nature or Israel's agrarian status, like Tu B'Shevat, Yom Ha'atzmaut, and Lag B'Omer.

# Orzo Salad with Roasted Carrots and Lentils

SERVES 4 TO 6 | DAIRY OR PAREVE

*I first tasted orzo in Israel, where it was served up along with the story of how Prime Minister David Ben Gurion asked the Osem company to create a product to replace rice, which was scarce. Italian orzo was also designed as a grain replacement, but for barley rather than rice. Tossed with lentils, roasted carrots, and olives, the tiny semolina pasta is perfect for picnics or barbecues; add feta or goat cheese to make it a meal.*

*Prep time: 10 minutes*
*Cook time: 30 minutes*

FOR THE SALAD

½ cup beluga (black) lentils or French green lentils, picked over and rinsed

4 large carrots, peeled and cut into ¼-inch dice

Extra-virgin olive oil for drizzling

1 cup uncooked orzo

¼ cup chopped green olives

FOR THE DRESSING

3 tablespoons extra-virgin olive oil

2 tablespoons red wine vinegar

1 tablespoon Dijon mustard

1 tablespoon freshly squeezed lemon juice

1 teaspoon balsamic vinegar

Sea salt or kosher salt

Freshly ground black pepper

½ cup crumbled feta cheese (optional)

MAKE THE SALAD: Preheat the oven to 400°F. In a medium saucepan, combine the lentils and 2 cups of water. Bring to a boil, reduce the heat, and simmer until the lentils are tender but still retain their shape, about 20 to 30 minutes, depending on the variety. Drain, rinse, and transfer to a large serving bowl.

Spread the diced carrots in a single layer on a rimmed baking sheet or 9-inch baking dish. Drizzle with a little olive oil and toss to coat. Roast in the preheated oven, stirring once or twice, until the carrots are tender and beginning to caramelize, about 15 to 20 minutes. Remove from the oven and set aside.

While the lentils and carrots are cooking, bring a pot of water to a boil, add the orzo, and cook for 8 to 10 minutes, or until tender. Drain well and add to the bowl with the lentils. Add the roasted carrots and olives, and stir to combine.

**MAKE THE DRESSING:** In a small bowl, whisk together the olive oil, red wine vinegar, mustard, lemon juice, and balsamic vinegar. Season with salt and pepper. Pour the dressing over the orzo salad and toss to coat. Add the feta, if using, and toss again.

**STORAGE:** *Leftover salad will keep, covered, in the refrigerator for 4 to 5 days.*

Note

In the United States, it's easiest to find Italian orzo, which is what I use in this recipe. For those living in Israel, the boat-shaped *ptitim* or *orez Ben Gurion*, which are essentially the same, make a good substitute. In either locale, you could substitute round Israeli couscous (pearl couscous, also called ptitim), prepared according to package directions.

# Quinoa with Arugula, Butternut Squash, and Citrus Vinaigrette

SERVES 4 TO 6 | PAREVE

*With vegetarian guests coming to one of our Seders, my mother started worrying about what they'd be able to eat—never mind the multicourse menu full of vegetarian options she always serves. Given my own vegetarian leanings, she charged me with making something "with protein." (Despite my nutrition degree, convincing Ema that vegetables and grains can provide plenty is a hard sell.) This festive quinoa dish satisfied her requirements—and our guests—and is now in year-round rotation as both a side dish and light main.*

*Prep time: 15 minutes*
*Cook time: 30 minutes*

### FOR THE SALAD

1 butternut squash, peeled, seeded, and cut into ½-inch cubes (about 1½ pounds)

2 tablespoons extra-virgin olive oil, plus 1 teaspoon, divided

1 cup quinoa, rinsed and drained

2 cups water or vegetable stock

2 cups baby arugula, rinsed and spun dry

¼ cup pomegranate seeds (optional)

### FOR THE VINAIGRETTE

Juice of 1 lime

2 tablespoons orange juice

2 tablespoons extra-virgin olive oil

1 tablespoon honey

1 large garlic clove, finely chopped

1 teaspoon ground cumin

½ teaspoon kosher salt or sea salt

MAKE THE SALAD: Preheat the oven to 425°F. Line a rimmed baking sheet or roasting pan with parchment or foil. Add the butternut squash to the pan, drizzle with 2 tablespoons of olive oil, and toss to coat. Spread the squash in a single layer, and roast in the preheated oven for 20 to 30 minutes, stirring once or twice, until the squash is tender and is caramelized in spots. Remove from the oven and set aside.

While the squash roasts, warm 1 teaspoon of olive oil in a medium saucepan set over medium-high heat. Add the quinoa and stir until toasted, about 1 to 2 minutes. Pour in the water or stock and bring to a boil. Reduce the heat and simmer, uncovered, until there is no more liquid in the pot and the quinoa is tender and translucent, with a small whitish ring around the middle of each grain, about 15 minutes.

*(CONTINUED)*

Remove from the heat, transfer the quinoa to a large bowl, and fluff with a fork to separate the grains. Add the arugula to the hot quinoa, and toss to wilt the greens. Gently fold in the roasted squash and any oil remaining in the pan.

MAKE THE DRESSING: In a small bowl, whisk together the lime juice, orange juice, olive oil, honey, garlic, cumin, and salt. Pour the dressing over the quinoa and toss to coat. Serve warm, at room temperature, or chilled, garnished with pomegranate seeds if using.

STORAGE: *Leftover salad will keep, covered, in the refrigerator for 3 to 4 days.*

# Farro Salad with Lemony White Beans, Roasted Red Peppers, and Cauliflower

SERVES 6 TO 8 | DAIRY OR PAREVE

*There's no clear consensus about the term "farro," but it's generally applied to emmer, spelt, and einkorn, ancient species of wheat that are making a comeback. Farro is most closely associated with Italian cuisine, but emmer and einkorn, which first grew wild in the Fertile Crescent, were staples in ancient Israel. This hearty salad will feed a crowd, which makes it ideal for entertaining or potlucks.*

*Prep time: 15 minutes*
*Cook time: 30 minutes*

### FOR THE SALAD

1½ cups semipearled farro

1 medium head cauliflower, trimmed and broken into bite-size florets

3 tablespoons extra-virgin olive oil, divided

2 large red bell peppers

1 (15-ounce) can white beans, drained and rinsed

Juice and zest of 1 large lemon

2 garlic cloves, finely chopped

2 tablespoons chopped flat-leaf parsley

1 teaspoon ground cumin

### FOR THE DRESSING

Freshly squeezed juice of 1 lemon

2 tablespoons extra-virgin olive oil

Sea salt

Freshly ground black pepper

Freshly shaved Parmesan cheese, preferably Parmigiano-Reggiano (optional)

**MAKE THE SALAD:** Preheat the oven to 425°F. Place the farro and enough cold water to cover by 2 inches in a large, heavy saucepan. Bring to a boil over high heat. Reduce the heat and simmer uncovered until the farro is tender but still al dente, about 18 to 20 minutes. Drain the farro and rinse under cold running water to stop the cooking process. Transfer to a large serving bowl.

While the farro is boiling, prepare the vegetables. Place the cauliflower florets in a single layer on a large, rimmed baking sheet. Drizzle with about 1 tablespoon olive oil and toss to coat. Rub the peppers with about 1 tablespoon olive oil and place in a baking dish. Roast the vegetables in the preheated oven, stirring the cauliflower and turning the peppers once or twice, until the florets are crisp-tender and beginning to caramelize, and the pepper skins char. This will take about 15 to 20 minutes for the cauliflower and 20 to 25 minutes for the peppers. Once roasted to specification, remove from the oven. *(CONTINUED)*

Place the beans in a medium bowl. Add the lemon juice and zest, 1 tablespoon olive oil, garlic, parsley, and cumin. When the peppers are cool enough to handle, peel, seed, and chop them, and add to the bean mixture. Add the cauliflower and bean mixture to the farro and toss together.

MAKE THE DRESSING: In a small bowl, whisk together the lemon juice and olive oil. Pour over the farro salad, and toss well. Season with sea salt and black pepper. Top with freshly shaved Parmesan cheese, if using.

STORAGE: *Leftover salad will keep, covered, in the refrigerator for 2 to 3 days.*

# Buckwheat Soba Salad

SERVES 4 | PAREVE

*When I was very little, I used to categorize certain things as "the same but different." My parents were entertained by the expression, which entered into the family parlance. Take soba: On the surface, it seems nothing like kasha, the toasted buckwheat groats that are a cornerstone of Russian Jewish cuisine. But since the noodles are made from the same grain (really a pseudocereal), and share kasha's distinctive flavor qualities, it's a prime example of "the same but different."*

*Prep time: 20 minutes*
*Cook time: 10 minutes*

### FOR THE SOBA SALAD

1 (8.8-ounce) package buckwheat soba

24 asparagus spears, trimmed of woody ends

1 yellow bell pepper, cored, seeded, and cut into thin strips

2 carrots, peeled and julienned

1 avocado, pitted and cut into ½-inch chunks

### FOR THE DRESSING

¼ cup tamari soy sauce (reduced sodium is fine)

¼ cup orange juice

2 tablespoons neutral-flavored oil, such as grapeseed or canola

2 tablespoons unseasoned rice vinegar

2 tablespoons pure maple syrup, preferably dark

2 teaspoons toasted sesame oil

1 teaspoon finely grated fresh ginger

For the garnish (optional)

Toasted sesame seeds

Toasted nori, cut into a chiffonade (thin ribbons)

**STORAGE:** *Leftover salad will keep, covered, in the refrigerator for up to 2 days.*

**MAKE THE SALAD:** Bring a large pot of water to a boil. Add the soba noodles and cook for 5 to 6 minutes, or until al dente. Drain and rinse under cold running water, then transfer the noodles to a large bowl.

To a large, deep skillet, add 1 inch of water and bring to a boil. Add the asparagus, reduce the heat, and simmer, turning the spears once, until crisp-tender and bright green, about 1 to 2 minutes. Drain and rinse the asparagus under cold running water to stop the cooking process. Chop the asparagus stalks into 1-inch pieces, leaving the tips whole. Add the asparagus, yellow pepper, and carrots to the soba, and toss together.

**MAKE THE DRESSING:** In medium bowl, whisk together the tamari, orange juice, oil, rice vinegar, maple syrup, sesame oil, and ginger. Pour half the dressing over the soba salad and toss to coat.

Top the soba with avocado, and serve with additional dressing on the side. Garnish with sesame seeds and nori, if using.

# Israeli Couscous with Garlic-Roasted Mushrooms

SERVES 4 TO 6 | PAREVE

*My grandmother adored my dad. It probably didn't hurt that they shared a mutual love of certain foods that my mom didn't care for, like mushrooms. Roasted with lots of garlic and a smattering of herbs, the earthy fungi make a delicious accent to toothsome Israeli couscous, and a perfect side dish for roasted chicken, fish, or brisket.*

*Prep time: 15 minutes*
*Cook time: 30 minutes*

### FOR THE MUSHROOMS

1½ pounds assorted mushrooms (such as shiitake, cremini, maitake, or chanterelle), cleaned, stemmed, and sliced

½ cup extra-virgin olive oil

6 to 8 garlic cloves, finely chopped

1½ teaspoons fresh oregano, or ½ teaspoon dried oregano

1 tablespoon fresh chopped basil, or 1 teaspoon dried basil

### FOR THE COUSCOUS

1 tablespoon extra-virgin olive oil

1½ cups Israeli couscous

1¾ cups vegetable broth or water

**MAKE THE MUSHROOMS:** Preheat the oven to 425°F. Line a large rimmed baking sheet with parchment paper. Place the mushrooms in a large bowl. Drizzle with the olive oil, add the garlic, oregano, and basil, and toss well to coat. Spread the mushrooms in a single layer on the baking sheet and roast in the preheated oven, stirring periodically, until they release their juices, shrink, and begin to caramelize, about 20 to 30 minutes.

**MAKE THE COUSCOUS:** While the mushrooms are roasting, warm the oil in a chef's pan or large saucepan over medium-high heat. Add the couscous and sauté until the grains begin to toast and turn golden, about 3 minutes. Pour in the water or broth and bring to a boil. Lower the heat, cover, and simmer until the liquid is absorbed and the couscous is al dente, about 12 minutes. Transfer to a large serving bowl.

Add the mushrooms to the couscous, along with any olive oil, herbs, and garlic remaining in the pan. Toss to combine. Serve warm.

# Couscous with Pistachios, Nectarines, and Herbs

SERVES 4 TO 6 | PAREVE

*I used to assume couscous would have been unfamiliar to my grandparents, whose non-Ashkenazi food wanderings skewed more Asian or European than Mizrahi. But through her recipe collection, I discovered that one of my grandmother's friends was an expert on Moroccan cuisine and had shared several very traditional recipes, including one for a vegetable and chicken tagine served over couscous. Making this couscous pilaf is much quicker, but it's got lots of textural interest, and complements a wide range of meals.*

*Prep time: 10 minutes*
*Cook time: 15 minutes*

### FOR THE COUSCOUS

1½ cups water

1 tablespoon extra-virgin olive oil

1½ cups whole-wheat couscous

2 large nectarines, pitted and chopped into ½-inch pieces

⅓ cup shelled, dry-roasted pistachios, preferably unsalted

2 scallions, white and light green parts only, thinly sliced into rounds

### FOR THE VINAIGRETTE

⅓ cup extra-virgin olive oil

2 tablespoons balsamic vinegar

¼ cup finely chopped fresh basil (from about 4 to 6 leaves)

2 tablespoons chopped fresh mint

¼ teaspoon fine sea salt

**MAKE THE COUSCOUS:** Bring the water to a boil in a medium saucepan. Add the olive oil, stir in the couscous, cover, and remove from the heat. Allow the couscous to rest, covered, for 5 minutes. Fluff the couscous grains with a fork, and transfer to a large bowl.

Add the nectarine pieces and pistachios to the couscous, and gently toss together.

**MAKE THE VINAIGRETTE:** In a small bowl, whisk together the olive oil, balsamic vinegar, basil, mint, and salt.

Pour the vinaigrette over the couscous and mix. Serve warm or at room temperature.

**STORAGE:** *Leftover salad will keep, covered, in the refrigerator for up to 5 days.*

# Parmesan-Quinoa Stuffed Mushrooms

SERVES 4 TO 6 | DAIRY

*When quinoa got the okay for Passover use, it was a game changer, especially for Ashkenazi vegetarians. Instead of leaden matzo stuffing, here was a light, grain-like side dish or filling for veggies. I like to give it some substance by mixing it with cheese and sautéed spinach, and using it to fill portobello caps or other hollowed-out veggies.*

*Prep time: 20 minutes*
*Cook time: 35 minutes*

### FOR THE MUSHROOMS

6 large portobello mushrooms, cleaned, stemmed, and wiped dry

2 tablespoons extra-virgin olive oil

1 tablespoon balsamic vinegar

### FOR THE QUINOA FILLING

1 cup quinoa, rinsed

2 cups water

1 tablespoon extra-virgin olive oil

1 large garlic clove, finely chopped

¼ cup grated Parmesan or Pecorino Romano cheese

⅓ cup shredded mozzarella cheese

2 ounces baby spinach, rinsed

¼ cup chopped pecans

Freshly ground black pepper

1½ cups marinara sauce (jarred or homemade)

Additional Parmesan cheese for serving (optional)

**MAKE THE MUSHROOMS:** Preheat the oven to 400°F. Line a rimmed sheet pan with parchment paper or foil. Arrange the mushroom caps on the baking sheet, gill side up. In a small bowl, whisk together the olive oil and balsamic vinegar, and drizzle evenly over the mushrooms. Bake in the preheated oven until the mushrooms soften and begin to release their juices, about 15 to 20 minutes. Remove and set aside, leaving the oven on.

**MAKE THE QUINOA:** While the mushrooms are baking, combine the quinoa and water in a medium saucepan. Bring to a boil over high heat, then reduce the heat and simmer until the water is absorbed and the quinoa is fluffy and translucent, with a thin, whitish ring visible around each grain, about 15 minutes.

Remove the quinoa from the heat. Stir in the olive oil, garlic, Parmesan, and mozzarella. Continue mixing until the cheese begins to melt. Stir in the baby spinach. When the leaves begin to wilt, fold in the pecans. Season to taste with black pepper.

Spoon the quinoa filling into the mushroom caps. Return to the oven and bake until heated through, about 15 minutes. About 5 minutes before the mushrooms are ready, place the marinara sauce in a small saucepan and warm over medium-high heat.

TO SERVE: Spoon about ¼ cup of marinara sauce in the centers of four to six plates. Top each with a quinoa-stuffed mushroom. Shave Parmesan over each, and spoon over a little additional sauce, if desired. Serve immediately.

STORAGE: *Leftovers will keep, covered, in the refrigerator for 1 to 2 days. Reheat in a 300°F oven before serving.*

Simple Swap

Instead of the mushrooms, try using the quinoa filling in hollowed-out zucchini or red bell peppers, or roasted, hollowed-out Japanese eggplant halves.

Butternut and Roasted Corn Chowder
with Garam Masala (page 139)

# CHAPTER SIX

# Soups

Could there be a more iconic image than that of a bubbe standing over a pot of matzo ball soup, ladling out the precious golden broth for a Shabbat or holiday dinner (or an under-the-weather loved one)? Maybe it's the idea that our grandmothers were inclined—whether by desire or necessity—to watch over pots of soup for hours, that I used to assume they were labor-intensive affairs that took hours to make. I've since learned what our grandmothers knew: Once you get them going, most soups aren't hard—or time consuming—to prepare. But they are elemental, comforting, and perfect for sharing with family and friends.

# Roasted Tomato Soup

*I was probably about four, and had spent the morning tromping around in the snow outside of my grandmother's apartment building. With my snowsuit sodden from making snow angels, we headed inside so she could deposit me in a warm bath. She returned a few minutes later with a lap tray holding a bowl of steamy tomato soup and crackers. I was thrilled by the treat, and by my grandmother's flouting the rule never to bring food into the bathroom. "This is different," she said. "You're in the tub." It was all very* Eloise at the Plaza. *When the memory sprang to mind while I was working on this book, I knew I had to pay homage to her with a tomato soup recipe. This one is beyond simple—canned fire-roasted tomatoes do the heavy lifting, flavor-wise—so you can throw it together quickly for snowy day warm-ups.*

*Prep time: 10 minutes*
*Cook time: 20 minutes*

2 tablespoons extra-virgin olive oil

1 large onion, chopped

1 large carrot, peeled and chopped

1 stalk celery, trimmed and chopped

3 large garlic cloves, chopped

1 (28-ounce) can diced fire-roasted tomatoes

2 cups vegetable stock

### How-To

Prefer a creamy soup? Stir a little cream, yogurt, or sour cream into the soup when serving.

In a stockpot or Dutch oven set over medium-high heat, warm the olive oil. Add the onion, carrot and celery and cook, stirring occasionally to keep from burning, until the onion turns soft and translucent, about 5 to 7 minutes. Add the garlic and sauté for 1 minute.

Add the tomatoes with their juice and the stock. Bring to a boil, reduce the heat, and simmer, partially covered, until the vegetables are tender, about 20 minutes.

Using an immersion or regular blender, purée the soup until partially or totally smooth, depending on your preference. (If you use a regular blender, be sure to hold the lid on to prevent the soup from flying out and burning you, and purée in batches if necessary.) Serve hot.

**STORAGE:** *Leftover soup will keep, covered, in the refrigerator for 3 to 4 days, or in an airtight container in the freezer for up to 3 months.*

# Classic Tomato Gazpacho

SERVES 4 TO 6 | PAREVE

*I'm not sure my grandmother would approve of the fact that I don't bother to blanch and peel my tomatoes before I make gazpacho. (Sometimes, I don't even seed them!) Of course, it's made in a blender instead of a mortar and pestle, so the skins aren't a big deal. The truth is, our family recipe isn't particularly Andalusian: It contains no bread, and gets a boost from tomato juice, which, though handy for covering for less-than-exceptional tomatoes, doesn't appear in traditional recipes. Some food historians believe the word* gazpacho *has etymological roots in the Hebrew word* gazaz, *which means "to shear" or cut into pieces. It's the sort of detail my grandmother would have loved and proudly shared whenever she served the soup.*

*Prep time: 15 minutes*
*Chilling time: 1 to 2 hours*

### FOR THE SOUP

2 pounds ripe tomatoes, cored and quartered

½ English cucumber, peeled and chopped

½ red bell pepper, cored, seeded, and chopped

½ green bell pepper, cored, seeded, and chopped

2 large garlic cloves, chopped

2 cups low-sodium tomato or vegetable juice

¼ cup extra-virgin olive oil

¼ cup red wine vinegar

Freshly ground black pepper

Sea salt

### FOR THE GARNISH

½ English cucumber, peeled and cut into ¼-inch dice

½ red bell pepper, cored, seeded, and cut into ¼-inch dice

½ green bell pepper, cored, seeded, and cut into ¼-inch dice

Small croutons, store-bought or homemade

**MAKE THE SOUP:** Working in batches if necessary, place the tomatoes, cucumber, red pepper, green pepper, garlic, and tomato juice into a blender jar or work bowl of a food processor. Purée until smooth. With the machine running, add the olive oil and vinegar through the lid and process until combined.

Transfer the gazpacho to a pitcher. Cover and chill in the refrigerator for 1 to 2 hours.

**MAKE THE GARNISH:** Place the diced cucumber, and red and green peppers for the garnish into individual serving bowls. Cover the bowls and refrigerate until ready to serve.

Just before serving, stir the gazpacho. Pour into cups or bowls. Set out the cucumbers, peppers, and croutons, and let diners add their own garnishes.

# Watermelon Gazpacho

SERVES 4 TO 6 | PAREVE

*Cold fruit soups resonate with memories of summer. This watermelon gazpacho is a refreshing riff on the more typical tomato version. It's a great way to use up an abundance of melon, and perfect for hydrating on a hot summer day.*

*Prep time: 20 minutes*
*Chilling time: 1 hour*

### FOR THE SOUP

5 cups cubed seedless watermelon

½ English cucumber, peeled and cut into chunks

½ red bell pepper, cored, seeded, and cut into chunks

1 medium shallot, peeled and chopped

1 large garlic clove, chopped

2 tablespoons extra-virgin olive oil

1 tablespoon balsamic vinegar

### FOR THE GARNISH

½ English cucumber, peeled and cut into ¼-inch dice

½ red bell pepper, cored, seeded, and cut into ¼-inch dice

Croutons, homemade or store-bought (optional)

Place the watermelon, cucumber, red pepper, shallot, and garlic into a blender jar or work bowl of a food processor. Pulse 3 to 4 times, then purée until smooth. Add the olive oil and vinegar, and purée for a few seconds to incorporate.

Pour the gazpacho into a large pitcher and cover with plastic wrap. Chill in the refrigerator for at least 1 hour, or until cold.

To serve, stir the gazpacho, and pour into bowls or cups. Set out the chopped cucumber, bell pepper, and croutons in individual serving bowls so diners can garnish their own soup. Or, mix the diced cucumber and pepper into the soup just before serving, and top each portion with a few croutons, if using.

# IN THE KITCHEN WITH
# KIM KUSHNER

*"What's the first thing you think about when you think about Juju?"*

*"Carrot soup."*

*"Juju's cookies."*

*"Sleepovers."*

*Those were the answers I received from my children when I asked them about their grandmother, my mom, whom everyone calls Juju. I'd never asked them this question before, but in reflecting on my own thoughts and memories surrounding my childhood, so much of my life revolved around food, and I wondered if they, too, made this association. I guess, as they say, the apple doesn't fall far from the tree.*

*My mother has built her life around feeding others. When she became a grandmother, this mission was taken to a whole new level. As I age, I've come to realize that my mother's obsession with "feeding the kids" is not so much about literally feeding my children as it is about feeding her own need to comfort, nourish, and protect her grandchildren. Perhaps she is even trying to fill a void she experienced in her own childhood, being raised without her parents and with so little from a very young age.*

*It's ironic that I've chosen a career in the food business, because it's not actually about the food. It's really about gathering as a family around the Shabbat table, it's about the connection between grandmother and grandchild while sipping tea and munching on Moroccan anise biscuits. It's about creating memories through taste and smell— this is the key that allows these memories to be recreated, re-experienced and passed on to future generations.*

*This story isn't an original tale. This is a story that's been told for years and years by people from various cultures, religions, and backgrounds. Food is the primary theme, serving as a link between the generations. I feel lucky to have my own strong version of this story. Juju is the main character; cookies and carrot soup play a strong role too. But in the end, it's the voices of those happy, nourished, loved children that will narrate.*

KIM KUSHNER is a private chef and cooking instructor of healthy, seasonal, and hearty kosher meals. She is the author of the cookbooks *The Modern Menu* and *The New Kosher*.

# Grandma Juju's Carrot Soup

PAREVE OR MEAT
*Serves 8 to 10*
*Prep Time: 10 minutes*
*Cook Time: 30 minutes*

2 tablespoons canola oil

4 yellow onions, peeled, trimmed, and diced

3 (1-pound) bags peeled baby carrots

1 (1-inch) piece ginger, peeled and minced

3 to 4 quarts vegetable broth or chicken stock

Kosher salt

Black pepper

In a large pot set over medium-high heat, warm the oil.

Add the onions, carrots, and ginger to the pot, and sauté until caramelized, about 10 minutes.

Pour in 3 quarts of the stock and bring to a boil. For a thinner soup, add up to 1 quart more stock. Reduce the heat to medium and simmer until the carrots are soft, about 20 minutes.

Using a hand immersion blender, purée the soup to your preferred consistency. If you use a countertop blender instead, work in batches. The soup will be hot and it's safer not to blend in its entirety. Only fill the blender about halfway, and be sure to hold the lid on the blender while puréeing. Season with salt and pepper.

# Parsley and Nutmeg Matzo Balls

MAKES 18 TO 24 MATZO BALLS | MEAT OR PAREVE

*The first time I encountered a softball-size matzo ball in a bowl of soup at a deli, I balked. I couldn't understand the appeal of getting one matzo ball instead of several. And the fluffy, broth-infused dumpling seemed, well, a little boring. That's because my reference point was my grandmother's nutmeg- and parsley-enhanced matzo balls. Hers toed the line between "sinker" and "floater," and had their own inherent flavor, so they had something to contribute to the broth. They're matzo balls with personality, and the ones we still make today.*

*Prep time: 20 minutes*
*Chilling time: 30 minutes to 1 hour*
*Cook time: 30 minutes*

4 eggs, lightly beaten

1 cup matzo meal

4 tablespoons schmaltz (rendered chicken fat), or olive oil

2 tablespoons finely chopped fresh parsley

½ teaspoon freshly grated or ground nutmeg

Chicken soup for serving (your recipe or page 136)

In a large bowl, mix the eggs, matzo meal, and schmaltz or oil. Stir in the parsley and nutmeg, mixing until the herbs and spices are evenly incorporated. Cover and chill for 30 minutes (for "floaters") to 1 hour (for "floater-sinker" hybrids).

Bring a large stockpot of salted water to a boil. With clean, oiled hands, scoop up a walnut-size piece of the chilled mixture and gently roll it between your palms to form a ball. Don't worry about forming a perfect sphere—the matzo balls will be fluffier if you don't compress them. Drop in the water, and continue forming matzo balls, taking care not to crowd the pot. (You may need to cook the matzo balls in batches). The matzo balls will sink when you first drop them in the water, but will rise to the top as they cook.

After you've added the matzo balls, give a gentle stir to dislodge any that may have stuck to the bottom. Return to a boil, lower the heat, and simmer, covered, for 25 to 30 minutes, until the matzo balls have lightened in color, are cooked through, and have doubled in size.

If you plan to serve the matzo balls right after preparing them, bring a pot of chicken soup to a simmer. When the matzo balls are ready, use a slotted spoon to transfer them to the simmering soup. Gently simmer, covered, until ready to serve.

**STORAGE:** *If you're preparing the matzo balls in advance, use a slotted spoon to transfer them to a baking dish. Cover and refrigerate for up to a day before reheating in simmering broth.*

# Golden Vegetable Broth with Dill Matzo Balls

SERVES 6 TO 8 | PAREVE

*My grandmother always served her matzo balls in chicken broth, and like many bubbes would have likely wondered why anyone would bother with anything else. During the years that my sister and I were vegetarian, we'd make a concession for Seder matzo ball soup. Then, one year we learned that a five-year-old Seder guest had just seen* Chicken Run *and declared himself a vegetarian. His mom called to see if there might be a way to accommodate the little matzo ball soup lover. I happily set to work on a soup he could enjoy without reservations. We've made a pot every year since.*

*Prep time: 30 minutes*
*Chilling time: 30 minutes*
*Cook time: 1 hour, 10 minutes*

## FOR THE BROTH

2 tablespoons extra-virgin olive oil

2 medium onions, chopped

6 medium carrots, peeled and cut into coins (about 1 pound)

4 celery stalks, trimmed and chopped (about ½ pound)

1 parsnip, peeled cut into coins

6 garlic cloves, smashed

1½ teaspoons fresh grated ginger

10 ounces cremini mushrooms, trimmed and chopped

1 medium zucchini, halved lengthwise and cut into half-moons

8 cups water

3 tablespoons fresh chopped basil, or 1 tablespoon frozen or dried basil

2 teaspoons sea salt or kosher salt

## FOR THE MATZO BALLS

2 tablespoons vegetable stock

4 eggs

1 cup matzo meal

¼ cup extra-virgin olive oil

2 tablespoons finely chopped fresh dill fronds

1 teaspoon sea salt or kosher salt

½ teaspoon ground ginger

**MAKE THE BROTH:** In a large stockpot set over medium-high heat, warm the oil. Add the onions, carrots, celery, and parsnip. Cook, stirring frequently so the vegetables don't brown, until the onions are soft and translucent, about 10 minutes.

Add the garlic and ginger. Sauté for 1 minute, or until fragrant. Add the mushrooms and cook, stirring frequently, until they release their juices, about 5 to 7 minutes. When most of the mushroom liquid has cooked off, add the zucchini and sauté until it begins to soften, about 3 to 5 minutes.

Add the water. Turn the heat to high and bring to a boil. Stir in the basil and salt. Lower the heat and simmer, partially covered, until broth is flavorful and golden, 45 to 60 minutes.

MAKE THE MATZO BALLS: While the soup is simmering, transfer a couple of tablespoons of the simmering stock from the stockpot to a small bowl to cool slightly. In a large bowl, beat the eggs. Mix in the matzo meal, olive oil, cooled vegetable stock, dill, salt, and ginger. Stir with a fork until well mixed. Cover and chill in the refrigerator for 30 minutes.

In the meantime, bring a large pot of salted water to a boil. When you are ready to make the matzo balls, scoop up a walnut-size piece of the chilled mixture with oiled hands and roll it into a ball between your palms, taking care not to compress it. Drop in the water, and continue forming matzo balls, being careful not to crowd the pot. You may need to cook the matzo balls in batches.

Gently stir to dislodge any matzo balls that may have stuck to the bottom. Return to a boil, lower the heat, and simmer, covered, for 25 to 30 minutes, until the matzo balls have lightened in color, cooked through, and are about doubled in size. When they are ready, you should be able to cut through one easily with the side of a spoon.

While the matzo balls are cooking, strain the broth. Set a large colander over another soup pot. Carefully pour the soup from the stockpot through the colander. If you prefer a very clear broth, line the colander with cheesecloth first.

Set aside some of the carrot and parsnip slices, then gently press on the vegetables in the colander with a spoon to extract the broth. If you don't have another soup pot, another option is set the colander over a large bowl and to transfer the veggies to it with a slotted spoon. Reserve some veggies, and press on the rest with the back of the spoon. Lift out the colander and pour the broth that has collected in the bowl back into the stockpot.

Return the reserved carrots and parsnips to the broth. If you'll be serving the soup right away, bring it to a simmer and add the prepared matzo balls. When the soup and matzo balls are hot, ladle into bowls and serve.

STORAGE: *You can make the broth 1 to 2 days in advance and refrigerate, covered, until ready to use. Or divide it among freezer-safe containers and freeze for up to 3 months. You can also prepare the matzo balls a day ahead. When they are cooked through, transfer them to an airtight container using a slotted spoon. Reheat in simmering broth.*

How-To

Skip straining the broth if you don't mind a heartier soup. Just ladle out the broth and spoon some of the vegetables into each bowl. It can be hard to find prepared vegetable broth that's kosher for Passover. If you rely on it for Pesach recipes, make a double batch of this and use it throughout the holiday.

# Ruby Chard and Lemongrass Schav with Herbed Sour Cream

SERVES 4 TO 6 | DAIRY

*My grandparents loved schav, an Eastern European sorrel soup. I never tasted my grandmother's homemade version, though she once offered up the jarred kind. Like so many of the convenience versions of her favorite foods, it looked totally unenticing to me. (The muddy green hue didn't help.) I've tried sorrel since, and enjoyed its puckery flavor, so I can understand schav's appeal. But it's surprisingly hard to find fresh sorrel in the market, so I set out to find an alternative. Chard seemed a good choice, and research revealed that it, too, was traditionally used to make schav. Lemongrass, a staple herb in Thai cuisine, echoes some of sorrel's citrusy notes. A bit of sour cream adds tang. I've updated the traditional topping with the addition of dill, scallion, and garlic. Enjoy it hot, or purée and serve well chilled, with a dollop of the sour cream sauce swirled in.*

*Prep time: 15 minutes*
*Cook time: 20 minutes*
*Chilling time: 4 hours*

## FOR THE SOUP

1 pound Swiss, ruby, or rainbow chard

1 stalk lemongrass, white and light green parts only

2 tablespoons unsalted butter

1 medium onion, finely chopped

4 cups vegetable stock or water

1 teaspoon salt (optional)

## FOR THE HERBED SOUR CREAM

1 cup sour cream

¼ cup finely chopped fresh dill

2 scallions, white and light green parts only, quartered lengthwise and finely chopped

2 garlic cloves, finely chopped

**MAKE THE SOUP:** Trim the tough ends from the chard and discard. Chop the tender stems, then stack and roll the leaves tightly. Cut the chard roll crosswise into thin ribbons, then lengthwise to chop into smaller pieces. Transfer to a bowl and set aside.

Trim off the bulb end of the lemongrass and remove any tough outer leaves. Use the side of a chef's knife to smash the lemongrass stalk. Finely mince the tender inner leaves, and cut any harder pieces into 2- to 3-inch pieces.

Set a large, heavy saucepan or Dutch oven over medium-high heat. Melt the butter, and add the minced lemongrass and onion. Sauté until the onion begins to soften, about 3 minutes. Add the chard and sauté until wilted, 2 to 3 minutes. Add the stock or water and salt (if using).

Bring to a boil, reduce the heat, then simmer, covered, until the greens are tender, about 15 minutes.

MAKE THE HERBED SOUR CREAM: While the soup is simmering, in a small bowl, mix the sour cream, dill, scallions, and garlic. Refrigerate, covered, until ready to use.

Serve the soup hot, as is. Or purée and refrigerate at least 4 hours. Either way, serve with a dollop of the herbed sour cream.

# "Emergency" Chicken Soup

SERVES 4 | MEAT

*I've got enough Jewish grandmother in me to think "chicken soup" when someone in the family catches a cold. And I've always hewn to the conventional wisdom that you can't make a good chicken soup without a whole chicken. But when my husband woke up with a nasty cold on a day too snowy for a chicken-buying trek, I threw caution to the wind, and some skinless, boneless chicken breasts in a pot. I expected failure, with maybe some decent poached chicken as a consolation prize. But we got a tasty soup, one that didn't require the skimming and straining of traditional chicken soup. It may not be your bubbe's rich* goldene yoich, *but it'll more than do in a pinch.*

*Prep time: 20 minutes*
*Cook time: 1 hour*

1 tablespoon extra-virgin olive oil

1 large onion, chopped

3 large carrots, peeled and chopped

2 celery stalks, trimmed and chopped

1 cup chopped butternut squash (from about a 3-inch piece, optional)

6 large garlic cloves, smashed

2 to 3 quarter-size slices fresh ginger, peeled

1½ pounds boneless, skinless chicken breasts

¾ cup dry white wine

Zest of 1 lemon, white pith removed, cut into 1-by-3-inch strips

2 teaspoons kosher salt or sea salt

¼ teaspoon turmeric

Freshly ground black pepper

### Tip

If you've got bone-in chicken parts on hand, you absolutely can use them. You'll get richer flavor, but the soup will take longer to cook, and you will need to skim the fat.

In a large stockpot or Dutch oven set over medium-high heat, warm the oil. Add the onion, carrots, and celery. Reduce the heat to medium-low and sweat the vegetables, stirring occasionally to prevent burning, until the onion is soft and translucent, about 5 to 7 minutes. Add the butternut squash (if using), garlic, and ginger, and sauté for 2 to 3 minutes more.

Add the chicken breasts, wine, and enough water to cover by 2 inches. Add the lemon zest, salt, turmeric, and a few grinds of black pepper. Raise the heat and bring to a boil. Reduce the heat, cover, and simmer until the chicken is cooked through and the broth is flavorful, about 45 minutes to 1 hour.

Remove the chicken breasts from the soup. When they are cool enough to handle, shred and return some or all of the meat to the soup, if you'd like. (You can also refrigerate the chicken and use it for wraps or chicken salad.) Simmer for a few more minutes to heat the shredded chicken through. Ladle into bowls and serve hot.

# Garlic, Ginger, and Turmeric Tonic Soup

SERVES 2 TO 4 | MEAT OR PAREVE

*I remember watching my Saba (grandfather) making a piece of knubble (garlic) bread at the kitchen table. He sliced a clove of garlic in half to expose the juice, then rubbed it on rye toast. "It's good for you," he said with a wink. "It's why he doesn't catch colds," my grandmother agreed. Now, if we start to feel under the weather, I reach for garlic. Sure, as a dietitian I've read many studies about the antibacterial, antiviral, and antifungal properties of the stinking rose. But it's garlic's fortifying flavor and savory aroma that makes it such a comforting addition to feel-better fare.*

*Prep time: 5 minutes*
*Cook time: 20 minutes*

4 cups chicken or vegetable broth

1 whole head garlic, cloves separated, smashed, peeled, and trimmed of hard ends

1 (½-inch) piece fresh ginger, peeled and finely grated or minced (about 1 tablespoon)

½ to 1 teaspoon ground turmeric

1 teaspoon miso paste (any variety, optional)

Sea salt

Freshly ground black pepper

Pour the broth into a medium saucepan. Add the garlic, ginger, and turmeric. Bring to a boil, reduce the heat, and simmer, partially covered, until the garlic is very tender, about 20 minutes. Remove from the heat and stir in the miso (if using).

With a regular or immersion blender, purée until smooth. Season with sea salt and freshly ground black pepper.

# Hearty Vegetable Soup with Farro

SERVES 4 TO 6 | PAREVE

*Vegetable soup has been a fixture at our fall and winter table for as long as I can remember. No matter what else would follow, the soup was bound to be my favorite part of the meal—especially if I scored a lot of lima beans. My mom still starts her soup with my grandmother's shortcut—a cellophane tube of split peas, beans, seasonings, and tiny pasta, courtesy of Manischewitz or Streit's. Considering how much else they'd toss in the pot, the mix was as superfluous as the pebble in* Stone Soup. *I skip it—and the inevitable undercooked split peas—and rely on whatever is in the fridge, pantry, and freezer.*

*Prep time: 15 minutes*
*Cook time: 45 minutes*

2 tablespoons extra-virgin olive oil

1 large onion, chopped

3 large carrots, peeled and diced

1 large parsnip, peeled and diced

3 large garlic cloves, chopped

4 cups vegetable stock

1 to 2 cups water

1 cup tomato sauce or 1 (14.5-ounce) can crushed or diced tomatoes

1 cup diced butternut or honeynut squash

½ cup fresh or frozen corn kernels

½ cup fresh or frozen peas

½ cup frozen baby lima beans

¼ cup semipearled farro

¼ cup green lentils (optional)

Sea salt

Freshly ground black pepper

Warm the olive oil in a large stockpot set over medium-high heat. Add the onion, carrots, and parsnip, and sauté until the onion softens and turns translucent, about 5 minutes. Add the garlic and sauté 1 minute more.

Pour the vegetable stock and 1 cup of water into the pot. Stir in the tomato sauce or tomatoes with their juice. Add the squash, corn, peas, lima beans, farro, and lentils (if using). Bring to a boil, reduce the heat, and simmer, partially covered, until the farro and lentils are tender, 30 to 40 minutes. Add extra water during cooking if you prefer a thinner soup.

STORAGE: *Leftover soup will keep, covered, in the refrigerator to 2 to 3 days. Or store in an airtight freezer container for up to 3 months. Leave a little headroom in the container to give the soup space to expand as it freezes. Leftover soup will thicken significantly in the fridge or freezer—just add additional water or stock when you reheat it.*

# Butternut and Roasted Corn Chowder with Garam Masala

SERVES 4 TO 6 | PAREVE

*My grandparents traveled around the world, and loved exploring the art, culture, and foods of foreign lands. They were also fascinated by the incredible diversity of Jewish diaspora culture, and I learned very early on that there were ancient Jewish communities around the world, with their own unique traditions and flavors. It was from my grandmother that I first learned of the Cochin Jews of India, and of the magnificence of the country. I imagine she would have loved having the easy access we now enjoy to spice blends like garam masala, so she could bring some of the flavors she enjoyed overseas to her own cooking.*

*Prep time: 15 minutes*
*Cook time: 30 minutes*

1 large or 2 medium butternut squash, peeled and seeded (4 to 5 pounds total)

1 tablespoon extra-virgin olive oil, plus extra for roasting the squash

2 medium onions, chopped (about 3 cups)

2 large garlic cloves, coarsely chopped

2½ teaspoons garam masala

4 cups vegetable stock or water

1 to 1½ teaspoons sea salt or kosher salt (optional)

Freshly ground black pepper

2 cups frozen corn kernels

Preheat the oven to 425°F. Cut about ⅔ of the butternut squash into 1-inch chunks, measuring and transferring to a large bowl as you go. You should have about 4 to 4½ cups of large squash chunks. Cut the remaining squash into ¼-inch dice. You should have about 2 cups of small dice; if there is extra squash, add it to the bowl of large pieces. You now have about 4 cups of squash cut into 1-inch chunks, plus 2 cups cut into ¼-inch cubes.

Place the small cubes in a roasting pan or rimmed baking dish. Drizzle with a little olive oil, toss to coat, and set aside.

In a large stockpot set over medium-high heat, warm the olive oil. Add the onions and sauté just until they turn soft and translucent, about 5 to 7 minutes. Add the garlic and garam masala and sauté until aromatic, about 1 minute more.

*(CONTINUED)*

Add the large squash chunks, stirring to combine with the onions and spices. Pour the stock or water into the stockpot. If you are using water, stir in 1 teaspoon of salt. (If you're using stock you may not need it; wait to taste the puréed soup before salting it.) Bring to a boil over high heat, then reduce the heat to medium-low and simmer for about 20 minutes, or until the squash is very tender.

When the soup starts to simmer, place the roasting pan with the diced squash in the preheated oven. Roast for 15 minutes, stirring midway through, or until the squash is tender and begins to caramelize. Add the corn kernels to the pan, mix to combine with the squash, and return to the oven to roast for 5 to 10 more minutes, or until the corn is hot and the vegetables are caramelized in spots. Remove from the oven and set aside.

With an immersion or regular blender, purée the soup until smooth. Season with salt and pepper. Stir in the roasted squash and corn. Or, for company-worthy presentation, ladle the soup into individual bowls and garnish with a spoonful of the roasted vegetables.

# Beluga Lentil Soup

SERVES 4 | PAREVE

*There were treasures in my grandmother's apartment. She let me paw through her jewelry box and handle trinkets from the breakfront. I was even allowed to peek in the bar, with its unusually shaped bottles of Scotch, Sabra, and intriguingly hued liquors. But the pantry held wonders too precious for me to touch. I remember my grandmother holding a jar of caviar and explaining that the tiny fish eggs were very fancy food for special occasions. Tasting was encouraged, but I couldn't hold the jar, lest I accidentally break it. I understand now that she wasn't showing me true caviar, which was neither kosher nor affordable. But it was the best she could get, and she was glad to have it. Whenever I use beluga lentils—tiny black legumes named for the delicacy they resemble—I think of her.*

*Prep time: 15 minutes*
*Cook time: 30 minutes*

1 tablespoon extra-virgin olive oil

1 small onion, chopped (about ½ cup)

1 large carrot, peeled and chopped (about ¼ cup)

1 medium red bell pepper, seeded and chopped (about ½ cup)

2 large garlic cloves, chopped

2 teaspoons garam masala

1 cup beluga lentils, rinsed and drained

4 ½ cups water

Sea salt

Freshly ground black pepper

In a large, heavy-bottomed saucepan, warm the oil over medium-high heat. Add the onion, carrot, and red pepper, and sauté until the onions begin to turn soft and translucent, about 5 minutes.

Add the garlic and sauté for 30 seconds, then add the garam masala and sauté for 30 seconds more, or until the mixture is aromatic and coated in the spices.

Add the water and stir in the lentils. Bring to a boil, then reduce the heat and simmer, partially covered, for 25 minutes. Season with sea salt and black pepper, then simmer uncovered until the lentils are tender, about 5 minutes more.

If desired, use an immersion or regular blender to purée about half of the soup. Stir the purée into the rest of the soup, and serve.

Salt-Crusted Branzino with Herbs (page 156)

# CHAPTER SEVEN

# Fish

Even as a small child, I knew my grandparents loved fish. I saw them order it in restaurants, and heard about dishes they'd enjoyed overseas. There were tales of my grandmother's mock crab soup—so convincing that no one with a basis for comparison believed it was kosher—but I never tasted it.

Only while compiling recipes for this book did I realize I rarely saw her cook fish, though the telltale splatters and matzo meal crumbs still wedged between pages 130 and 131 of her *Settlement Cookbook* are evidence that she did, and often. Maybe because her kids weren't fans, she didn't serve it at family gatherings, or pass down her recipes. But her love of the piscine lives on in her grand- and great-grandchildren. And fish are great for kosher keepers; there are hundreds of kosher species, and they don't require shechita. So even in places where it's tough to track down kosher meat or poultry, fish can stay on the menu.

# Penne with Tuna, Artichokes, and Capers

SERVES 4 TO 6 | PAREVE

*My grandmother was a master at doctoring convenience foods, so even if she wasn't cooking entirely from scratch, it seemed as if she had. In this recipe, I've used a bunch of her tricks—from adding wine to ready-made tomato sauce, to jazzing things up with added spices, a squeeze of citrus, or some capers to make a simple meal more interesting and satisfying. Combining pasta (our busy weeknight go-to) with tuna (my grandmother's) seemed a great way to pay homage to her flair for making any dish— even the ones with shortcuts—her own.*

*Prep time: 10 minutes*
*Cook time: 25 minutes*

1 pound penne

2 tablespoons extra-virgin olive oil, plus extra for the pasta

3 large garlic cloves, chopped

1 pound frozen artichoke hearts or bottoms

3 tablespoons olives, pitted and coarsely chopped

3 tablespoons capers, drained

Pinch red pepper flakes

Freshly squeezed juice of ½ lemon

1 (24-ounce) jar good quality marinara sauce

Splash dry red wine

2 (5- or 6-ounce) cans tuna packed in olive oil or water, drained and flaked into large chunks

Bring a large pot of water to a boil. Add the pasta and cook according to package directions until it's al dente, about 9 to 11 minutes. Drain but do not rinse. Transfer to a large bowl and drizzle with olive oil.

While the pasta is boiling, prepare the artichokes. In a cast iron or other heavy skillet, warm the olive oil over medium-high heat. Add the garlic and sauté for 30 seconds. Add the artichokes and cook, stirring occasionally so the garlic doesn't burn, until the artichokes begin to brown in spots, about 5 to 7 minutes. Turn and cook on the other side until cooked through and caramelized, about 4 to 5 minutes more. Add the olives, capers, and red pepper flakes and sauté for 2 to 3 minutes. Squeeze the lemon juice over the mixture and sauté for 1 minute more. Remove from the heat and set aside.

In a large saucepan, combine the sauce with a generous splash of dry red wine. Heat over medium-high heat, then reduce the heat and simmer for 3 to 5 minutes. Add the pasta to the sauce, stir to coat, and remove from the heat.

Serve the pasta in shallow bowls topped with the artichoke mixture and the tuna.

STORAGE: *Leftover pasta will keep, covered, in the refrigerator for 2 to 3 days.*

Simple Swap

This recipe is a loose template, easily customized with your favorite additions. Substitute seared fresh tuna or grilled salmon for the canned tuna, use sautéed spinach or broccoli rabe instead of artichokes, or skip the fish and top with grated Parmesan cheese or cubes of fresh mozzarella (which, of course, will make this a dairy dish).

# Old-School Salmon Cakes

MAKES 8 TO 10 | PAREVE

*Aside from her chopped herring, this is the only recorded fish recipe I have from my grandmother. Of course, the card was pretty nonspecific—there were suggested seasoning options, but no specifics about how much she'd use of what. Both my mother and my aunt say they didn't pay much attention to what went in them, because they weren't especially interested in eating them. I take the nebulous notes as permission to tailor the herbs and spices to whatever we're in the mood for. You can change up this recipe yourself by subbing canned tuna for the salmon, experimenting with the seasonings, or by swapping panko bread crumbs for the matzo meal.*

*Prep time: 10 minutes*
*Cook time: 15 minutes*

2 (5- to 6-ounce) cans skinless, boneless salmon, drained

1 small onion, finely minced (about ½ cup)

1 tablespoon freshly squeezed lemon juice

1 tablespoon mayonnaise

2 tablespoons finely chopped fresh dill or parsley (optional)

1 teaspoon Old Bay or Cajun seasoning (optional)

½ teaspoon garlic powder

A few dashes Worcestershire sauce

Sea salt or kosher salt

Freshly ground black pepper

2 large eggs, lightly beaten

¼ cup matzo meal, plus extra for dredging

Olive oil, canola oil, or grapeseed oil

Preheat the oven to 250°F. Line a baking sheet with parchment, and a plate with paper towels.

In a large bowl, combine the salmon, onion, lemon juice, and mayonnaise. Mix well. Add the dill or parsley and/or Old Bay (if using), the garlic powder, and Worcestershire sauce. Stir to combine, and season with salt and pepper. Taste the mixture and adjust the seasoning— the salmon should be slightly more seasoned than you'd like the cakes to be, as the eggs and matzo meal will mellow the flavor. Stir in the eggs and matzo meal, mixing until well combined.

Pour some matzo meal onto a plate. With clean hands, form the salmon mixture into patties, then dredge in the matzo meal. Place the patties on a plate.

Add between ¼ and ½ inch of oil into a cast iron or other heavy skillet set over medium-high heat. When the oil is hot and shimmery, add 3 to 4 salmon cakes, taking care not to crowd the pan. Cook for 4 to 5 minutes per side, or until the cakes are golden brown and cooked through.

Transfer the cakes to a plate lined with paper towels briefly to drain extra oil, then place them on the baking sheet and slide into the oven to keep warm while you pan-fry the rest of the cakes.

**STORAGE:** *Refrigerate, wrapped in foil, for up to 2 days. Serve warm or chilled.*

How-To

If you'd rather not fry, you can bake the cakes instead. Pour a little olive oil in a shallow bowl, quickly dip both sides in the oil, then bake at 350°F on a parchment-lined baking sheet for 25 to 30 minutes, turning them over halfway through.

# Pistachio and Mint-Crusted
# Wild Salmon with Tzatziki

SERVES 4 | DAIRY

*When my mother was a child, she and my grandmother were taking a shopping break in a department store café when they were approached by a Turkish sea captain, hoping to chat with a countrywoman during his brief time in port. He refused to believe they were American, and insisted that at some point, the family must have hailed from Turkey. This sort of thing happened to my grandmother all of the time, and as proud as she was of her Jewish heritage, she enjoyed being mistaken for Italian or Greek, because it gave her the chance to dish about cross-cultural commonalities, in her life and in her cooking. As far as I know, she never made tzatziki, that delicious Greek sauce made of yogurt, cucumber, and garlic. But the elements of this dish would have been as familiar to her own bubbe as to a Greek yia-yia—and in wonderful, capable hands either way.*

*Prep time: 10 minutes*
*Cook time: 15 minutes*

FOR THE TZATZIKI

½ large cucumber, peeled and seeded

1 (6-ounce) container plain regular
   or low-fat yogurt

1 tablespoon freshly squeezed lime juice
   (from about ½ a lime)

1 large garlic clove, finely chopped

Pinch of salt

Pinch of cayenne pepper

FOR THE FISH

¼ cup shelled unsalted pistachios

¼ cup panko bread crumbs (or regular
   unseasoned bread crumbs)

1 tablespoon (packed) fresh mint leaves,
   rinsed and dried (about 15 mint leaves)

1½ pounds wild salmon fillets, cut into four
   6-ounce portions, skin removed

Extra-virgin olive oil for drizzling

Lemon wedges for serving (optional)

*(CONTINUED)*

**MAKE THE TZATZIKI:** Set a box grater over a colander and coarsely grate the cucumber. Press on the grated cucumber to extract as much liquid as possible, then add the drained cucumber to the yogurt. Add the lime juice, garlic, salt, and cayenne. Cover and refrigerate until ready to use. You can make the tzatziki up to 6 hours ahead.

**MAKE THE FISH:** Preheat the oven to 400°F. Line a sheet pan with parchment paper, or lightly oil a baking dish. In a food processor fitted with an S blade, combine the pistachios, bread crumbs, and mint. Pulse several times to finely chop, taking care not to process the mixture into a paste. Alternatively, you can finely chop the mixture by hand.

Place the salmon fillets in the prepared pan. Evenly divide the pistachio-mint mixture among the salmon fillets, patting gently to evenly cover the top of each. Lightly drizzle with olive oil.

Bake in the preheated oven until the salmon is opaque throughout and the topping is golden brown, about 10 to 15 minutes, depending on the thickness of the fillets.

Serve with the tzatziki and lemon wedges, if using.

# Orange Dijon Salmon

SERVES 4 | PAREVE

*Our Shabbat dinner menus vary a lot, but the one near-constant is salmon. My kids adore it, and have come to expect it as part of the meal, so it's become a new tradition for us. I think my grandmother would be proud—or at least relieved—that her great-grandkids turned out to have as much of an affinity for fish (especially one so rich in omega-3 fatty acids) as she and my grandfather had. This recipe is easily multiplied for company. Ask your fishmonger to cut a large fillet into 4- to 6-ounce individual portions if you prefer to serve clean cuts to each guest.*

*Prep time: 5 minutes*
*Cook time: 15 to 20 minutes*

1 to 1¼ pounds center-cut salmon fillet, skin removed

2 tablespoons tamari soy sauce (reduced sodium is okay)

2 tablespoons pure maple syrup

1 tablespoon orange juice

1 tablespoon Dijon mustard

1 teaspoon toasted sesame oil

### How-To

If you take the time to marinate the fish in advance, you can also remove it from the marinade and roast it on a parchment-lined baking sheet. This method yields a firmer, less saucy fillet. Want extra sauce on the side? Double the marinade, use half on the fish, and simmer the rest in a small saucepan set over medium-high heat until it reduces and thickens slightly.

Preheat the oven to 425°F. Place the salmon in a baking dish slightly larger than the fillet.

In a small bowl, whisk together the tamari, maple syrup, orange juice, mustard, and sesame oil. Pour over the fish. You can cook the fish right away, or cover and marinate in the refrigerator for up to 4 hours. (If you're prepping the fish ahead, wait to preheat the oven until you're nearly ready to cook.)

Roast the fish in the preheated oven, basting once or twice, until it is opaque throughout, about 12 to 18 minutes, depending on the thickness of the fillet.

STORAGE: *Leftover fish will keep, covered, in the refrigerator for 1 to 2 days.*

# Sole with Spinach, Lemon, and Capers

SERVES 4 AS A MAIN COURSE, 8 AS AN APPETIZER | DAIRY OR PAREVE

*My grandparents loved fish of all sorts, but according to my Ema, one of my grand-mother's favorite go-to preparations was very simple. She'd dot flounder or sole fillets with butter, add a squeeze of lemon and some capers, and broil. This recipe is a nod to hers, with a little sautéed fresh spinach thrown in for good measure.*

*Prep time: 10 minutes*
*Cook time: 25 minutes*

2 tablespoons extra-virgin olive oil, plus extra for drizzling on fish

3 large garlic cloves, finely chopped

10 ounces baby spinach, rinsed but not dried

8 sole or flounder fillets (about 1½ to 2 pounds)

Kosher salt or sea salt

Freshly ground black pepper

1 tablespoon butter (optional)

Juice of 1 lemon

2 tablespoons dry white wine

2 tablespoons capers

### Simple Swap

Instead of capers, try topping the baked rolls with dukkah, an Egyptian blend of nuts, herbs, and spices. Find it in some specialty and gourmet supermarkets, international markets, or online.

Preheat the oven to 400°F. Butter or oil a 2-quart baking dish.

In a chef's pan or large skillet, warm the oil over medium-high heat. Add the garlic and sauté until fragrant, about 1 minute. Add the baby spinach (with any water still clinging to the leaves) to the pan. Sauté until the leaves wilt and collapse on themselves, turn a deep, vibrant green, and most of the liquid in the pan cooks off, 3 to 5 minutes. Remove from the heat.

Lay a sole fillet on a work surface, pretty side down. Place ⅛ of the spinach at the wider end of the fillet. Starting at the spinach end, roll up the fillet, and place seam side down in the baking dish. Repeat with the remaining fish and spinach.

Season the rolls with a couple pinches salt and a few grinds pepper. Dot with butter (if using) or drizzle with more olive oil. Squeeze the lemon over the fish, then drizzle with the wine. Top evenly with the capers.

Cover the dish with foil, and bake in the preheated oven for 15 to 20 minutes, or until the fish is opaque and cooked through. Serve immediately. Serve one roll per person as a first course, or two as an entrée.

# Moroccan-Spiced Cod with Oranges and Olives

SERVES 4 | PAREVE

*Chalk it up to hearing about my parents' trip to Spain and Morocco when I was a baby (the only time, as parents, they vacationed sans kids), but I was always curious about those countries. During a summer stint as a camp counselor in Kiryat Gat, Israel, I lived with a Moroccan-Jewish family, and fell in love with the cuisine. When I first made my own ras el hanout for potato latkes, I was so enamored with the spice blend that I looked for as many ways to use it as I could. I sprinkled it on everything from popcorn to roasted potatoes, but one of my favorite ways to use it may be in this oven-roasted cod recipe. The interplay among the briny olives, sweet orange, and the ras el hanout gives the dish complex flavor belied by its ease of preparation.*

*Prep time: 10 minutes*
*Cook time: 20 minutes*

4 cod fillets, skin removed (1¼ to 1½ pounds total)

1½ tablespoons ras el hanout (page 98)

Juice of 1 large orange, about ¼ to ⅓ cup

3 tablespoons extra-virgin olive oil

⅓ cup good quality pitted black or green olives, or a mix

2 tablespoons finely chopped fresh parsley

Lemon wedges for serving

Preheat the oven to 425°F. Place the cod fillets in a baking dish. Divide the ras el hanout evenly among the fillets. Gently rub the top of each to coat the fish evenly with the spices.

In a small bowl, whisk together the orange juice and olive oil. Pour over the fish, then top the fillets evenly with the olives.

Bake in the preheated oven until the fish is opaque and flakes easily with a fork, about 15 to 20 minutes, depending on the thickness of the fillets.

Sprinkle with the chopped parsley. Serve with lemon wedges.

# Black Bass with Burst Cherry Tomatoes and Herbs

SERVES 4 | PAREVE

*My grandmother loved tomatoes of all types, and taught my mom and aunt that juicy ripe beefsteaks were best for eating out of hand, and that Romas were ideal for slow-cooked dishes. I'm sure she'd have loved these little quick-roasted tomatoes too. High heat bursts the skins, intensifies the tomato flavor, and renders the texture almost confit-like. The result is the perfect condiment for pan-roasted fish.*

*Prep time: 10 minutes*
*Cook time: 20 minutes*

1 pint grape or cherry tomatoes, halved if large

2 tablespoons extra-virgin olive oil

2 garlic cloves, finely chopped

Kosher salt or sea salt

Freshly ground black pepper

1 tablespoon canola or grapeseed oil

4 (4- to 6-ounce) skin-on black bass fillets, or other firm-fleshed white fish such as grouper, mahi mahi, or snapper

Cajun spice, Old Bay, or other favorite spice blend (optional)

4 to 6 leaves fresh basil, cut into chiffonade

Preheat the oven to 425°F. Line a rimmed baking sheet with parchment paper and set aside. Place the tomatoes in a baking dish just large enough to hold them in a single layer. Toss with the olive oil and garlic. Season with a pinch of salt and a couple of grinds of black pepper. Roast in the preheated oven to 15 to 20 minutes, shaking the pan once or twice during cooking, until the tomatoes burst and begin to soften. Remove from the oven and set aside. Lower the oven temperature to 400°F.

Place a large, heavy cast iron or stainless steel skillet over medium-high heat for about 1 minute, or until the pan is very hot. Add the oil and warm until it starts to shimmer. Carefully place 2 fish fillets in the pan skin-side down. With a flexible spatula, press down on the fillets for about 1 minute to keep them from curling, and to ensure the skin remains in contact with the pan.

Allow the fillets to cook undisturbed for 4 to 5 minutes, or until the skin browns and turns crisp and the sides of the fish begin to turn opaque. Sprinkle the top of each fillet with a pinch salt and/or a favorite spice blend, if using. Carefully flip each fillet and continue cooking for 1 to 3 minutes more, or until the fish is opaque throughout.

Transfer the fillets, skin-side up, to the prepared baking sheet. If the fillets are thick, use a fork to check whether they are cooked through. If they are not, slide the baking sheet into the oven and allow to continue cooking while you pan sear the remaining fillets. If the fillets are cooked through, turn off the oven; the residual heat will keep the fish warm while you cook the remaining fillets.

Serve the fillets skin-side up or down, depending on your preference, with a generous spoonful of roasted tomatoes, topped with the basil chiffonade.

How-To

If you have two skillets, you can cook all of the fillets at the same time. And if your skillets are ovenproof, you can pop them right in the oven to finish off cooking the fish, if necessary.

# Salt-Crusted Branzino with Herbs

SERVES 4 TO 6 | PAREVE

*Though she'd plotz if she saw how much salt was involved in the preparation of this recipe, my grandmother was not afraid of whole fish. Like countless bubbes, she was the sort who'd buy them live from the fishmonger, and let them swim in the bathtub before thwacking them on the head and turning them into gefilte fish. This understandably scarred my mom and aunt, who never make gefilte fish from scratch and don't much care for being served fish with the head still on. But this recipe won them over, and I'm sure my grandmother would have loved it too. The salt crust insulates the herb-stuffed fish, allowing them to steam in their own little ovens, but doesn't turn the flesh salty.*

*Prep time: 15 minutes*
*Cook time: 35 to 40 minutes*

6 to 7 cups flaked kosher salt or coarse crystal sea salt

½ to ¾ cup water

2 to 3 whole branzino, about 1 to 1¼ pounds each, cleaned

2 to 3 medium regular or Meyer lemons, scrubbed and cut into rounds

3 sprigs fresh rosemary

1 bunch fresh oregano

Fresh dill or thyme (optional)

Freshly ground black pepper

Extra-virgin olive oil (optional)

Preheat the oven to 425°F. In a medium bowl, mix the salt with ½ cup of water. The salt should feel like wet sand. If it is too dry, add more water, a tablespoon or two at a time, until it reaches the right consistency.

In a roasting pan large enough to hold the fish, add about ¼ of the salt mixture, or enough to cover the bottom of the pan to make a bed for the fish.

Stuff each fish with a few lemon rounds, a sprig of rosemary, a couple sprigs of oregano, and dill or thyme if using (Fig. 1). Lay the fish side by side in the roasting pan, leaving about an inch between fish.

Season the fish with pepper. Take a handful of the salt mixture and spread it over one of the fish. Use your hands to mold the salt into a crust, using some of the salt from beneath the fish to cover the sides. Repeat with the remaining fish and salt.

Bake in the preheated oven for 35 to 40 minutes. The crust should be firm, and the fish flaky and opaque. To check for doneness, crack a little bit of the salt near the side of the fish, and pull back a little of the skin—it should separate easily from the flesh. You can also check it with an instant-read thermometer, which should register 140°F.

Allow the fish to rest for 5 to 10 minutes. Crack the salt crust with the side of a spoon (Fig. 2), and pull it away from the fish (Fig. 3). Drizzle with a little extra virgin olive oil if you'd like, and dig in.

How-To

You can use the salt crust method for other whole fish, such as snapper or bass. If you have a grill, you can skip the salt crust all together, and cook the lemon and herb-stuffed fish outdoors over a charcoal or gas fire.

Cranberry Horseradish Brisket (page 178)

# CHAPTER EIGHT

# Poultry and Meat

For my grandmothers, meat was about elemental nourishment, and it made a meal. Bubbe preferred to select live chickens and take them to the shochet herself. My grandmother kashered her meat on a rack by the sink (something kosher butchers now do as a convenience), and taught me to crack bones to get at the marrow—the best part. They relished dishes like pickled tongue, and liver and onions. And though I don't plan most meals around meat as they did, I try to emulate their respect for the animals that provided it whenever I prepare or eat it. I seek out organic or grass-fed kosher meat and poultry, save carcasses for stock, and aim to make recipes so delicious that nothing gets wasted.

# Citrus Chicken with Clementine Salsa

SERVES 4 | MEAT

*When I was little, the East Coast winters were occasionally punctuated by the arrival of a box of clementines, ruby grapefruits, or best of all, Israeli Jaffa oranges that some far-flung friend would send to my grandparents. At the time, these citrus varieties were exotic enough to give as gifts. Now their year-round availability means I can add their burst of sunshine to summer's grilled or winter's baked chicken.*

*Prep time: 20 minutes*
*Marinate time: 30 minutes to 6 hours*
*Cook time: 15 minutes for grilling, 35 minutes for roasting*

### FOR THE CHICKEN

¼ cup orange juice

2 tablespoons freshly squeezed lemon juice

1 tablespoon extra-virgin olive oil

2 large garlic cloves, chopped

Generous pinch of saffron threads

¼ teaspoon sea salt or kosher salt

Freshly ground black pepper

1½ pounds boneless, skinless chicken breasts

### FOR THE CLEMENTINE SALSA

4 clementines, peeled and chopped

¼ cup finely chopped red onion

2 tablespoons extra-virgin olive oil

1 to 2 tablespoons lime juice or
    clementine juice

2 large garlic cloves, finely chopped

¼ teaspoon kosher salt or sea salt

¼ cup flat-leaf parsley, finely chopped

**MAKE THE CHICKEN:** In a medium bowl, whisk together the orange juice, lemon juice, olive oil, garlic, saffron, salt, and a few grinds of black pepper. Place the chicken breasts in a baking dish or large plastic zipper-top bag. Pour the marinade over the chicken, cover or seal, and refrigerate for at least 30 minutes up to 6 hours.

**MAKE THE SALSA:** While the chicken marinates, combine the chopped clementines, onion, olive oil, lime or clementine juice, garlic, and salt, in a medium bowl. Stir in the parsley, cover, and refrigerate until ready to serve.

To cook outdoors, oil the clean grate of a gas or charcoal grill and preheat to medium-high. Remove the chicken from the marinade and grill, turning once, until it is cooked through, and an instant-read thermometer reads 165°F, about 4 to 6 minutes per side.

To cook indoors, oil a cast iron grill pan, preheat over medium-high heat, then add the chicken breasts in a single layer, taking care not to crowd the pan; work in two batches—or two pans—if necessary. Cook, turning once or twice, until the chicken is completely cooked through, the juices run clear, and an instant-read thermometer inserted in the thickest part of the meat reads 165°F. Or, preheat the oven to 350°F. Place the chicken and marinade in a baking dish just large enough to hold the chicken in a single layer, and roast uncovered, basting once or twice, until cooked through, about 30 to 35 minutes.

While the chicken is cooking, remove the salsa from the refrigerator and allow to come to room temperature. Serve the chicken hot, topped with a spoonful of the salsa.

STORAGE: *Leftover chicken will keep, well wrapped, in the refrigerator for 2 to 3 days. Store the salsa in a separate covered container.*

Tip

The salsa is also great on grilled fish, or as a topper for a tofu rice bowl.

# Pomegranate-Lacquered Roast Chicken

SERVES 4 | MEAT

*Duck à l'orange, I learned from my grandmother, was very delicious, very French, and exactly the sort of thing to order if we got dressed up to dine at a fancy restaurant. She loved telling the story of when my mother was small and a very picky eater, and they went out to eat. Claiming she wasn't hungry, Ema proceeded to devour her father's duck when it arrived at the table. I very much wanted to pay homage to my grandmother's role in my own early love of duck. But thanks to the cold water processing that tends to leave kosher ducks riddled with pinfeathers, I thought better of that plan. Instead, I treated a whole chicken to the pomegranate reduction intended for birds of another feather.*

*Prep time: 15 minutes*
*Cook time: 1 hour, 30 minutes*

### FOR THE CHICKEN

1 yellow or Spanish onion, peeled, halved, and sliced

1 (3½- to 5-pound) roasting chicken

½ lemon or orange

Extra-virgin olive oil

Kosher salt or sea salt

Freshly ground black pepper

¼ to ½ teaspoon cinnamon

¼ to ½ teaspoon ground cumin

Pomegranate seeds for garnish (optional)

### FOR THE POMEGRANATE REDUCTION

1 cup pomegranate juice

2 tablespoons honey

1 tablespoon brown sugar

2 tablespoons tamari soy sauce

**MAKE THE CHICKEN:** Preheat the oven to 450°F. Spread the onions in a roasting pan. If there are any giblets or the neck in the chicken cavity, remove and discard them, or freeze for stock if desired. Pluck any pinfeathers, then rinse the chicken inside and out with cold water and pat dry.

Place the chicken on top of the onions, breast up. Place the halved lemon or orange in the cavity, and truss the chicken if desired. Drizzle a little olive oil over the chicken and massage it all over the skin. Season with a pinch of salt, a few grinds of black pepper, cinnamon, and cumin, and rub all over the chicken. Let the chicken rest briefly while you make the pomegranate reduction.

MAKE THE POMEGRANATE REDUCTION: In a medium saucepan, combine the pomegranate juice, honey, brown sugar, and tamari. Bring to a boil, reduce the heat, and simmer, uncovered, until the sauce is slightly reduced and thickened, about 10 minutes. Remove from the heat, pour half into a small serving pitcher or bowl, and set aside.

Place the chicken in the preheated oven and roast for 10 minutes. Lower the temperature to 425° and roast for 30 minutes. Brush the chicken with some of the pomegranate reduction from the saucepan. Continue roasting, basting with pan juices and brushing once or twice more with pomegranate reduction, until cooked through, 20 to 40 minutes, depending on the size of the chicken. The chicken is done when the juices run clear, the legs wiggle freely in their joints, and a meat thermometer inserted into the thickest part of the thigh reads 165°F.

Remove the chicken from the oven, tent with foil, and allow it to rest for 10 minutes before carving. Garnish with pomegranate seeds if using, and serve with the reserved pomegranate reduction on the side.

# Marmalade-Roasted Chicken with Potatoes

SERVES 4 TO 6 | MEAT

*Before boneless, skinless chicken breasts became a supermarket mainstay, my grand-mother made her chicken with a whole or cut-up fryer. When ditching fat was the nutritional vogue, she made the switch. But bone-in chicken is undeniably juicier and more flavorful, and nothing beats tender potatoes roasted in the schmaltzy pan drippings. Happily, nutrition science has a more nuanced understanding of the potential benefits of dietary fat, and the roast chicken is vindicated. Inspired by my grandmother's love of marmalade, I used it in this dish to impart citrusy notes to the savory marinade.*

*Prep time: 15 minutes*
*Cook time: 1 hour, 15 minutes*

1 medium onion, peeled and sliced

1 pound waxy potatoes, such as Yukon Gold, halved (or quartered if large)

1 (3½- to 4-pound) chicken, cut in 8 pieces

3 tablespoons thick-cut marmalade

3 tablespoons extra-virgin olive oil

Juice of 2 Meyer lemons or 1 large regular lemon

1½ tablespoons tamari soy sauce (reduced sodium is fine)

1½ tablespoons unseasoned rice vinegar or white wine vinegar

**STORAGE:** *Leftovers will keep, covered, in the refrigerator for 2 to 3 days.*

Preheat the oven to 425°F. Spread the onions in the bottom of the roasting pan and arrange the potatoes around the perimeter of the pan. Lay the chicken pieces on top of the onions in a single layer.

In a medium bowl, mix together the marmalade, olive oil, lemon juice, tamari, and vinegar. Pour evenly over the chicken.

Roast in the preheated oven, basting the chicken and potatoes every half hour, until the potatoes are tender and the chicken skin is golden brown, the juices run clear, and an instant-read thermometer inserted in the thick-est part of a thigh and breast reads 165°F, about 1 hour to 1 hour, 15 minutes. Serve the chicken hot, with potatoes on the side.

Tip

Want saucier chicken? Spoon more marmalade on the chicken when you baste at the 45-minute mark.

# Easy Apricot Chicken

SERVINGS VARY | MEAT

*There are no specific measurements in this recipe, but don't let that scare you—the simplicity and easy adaptability are part of its beauty. And since my mom has carried on her mom's tradition and made it for years for Shabbat and holidays, it's definitely time-tested! Make as much or as little chicken as you need—if you're cooking for a crowd, figure half a pound per person. Some will eat more, some less, so there should be enough for everyone.*

*Prep time: 10 minutes*
*Cook time: 35 minutes*

Boneless, skinless chicken breasts
Garlic powder
Paprika
Kosher salt or sea salt
Freshly ground black pepper
Apricot preserves
Extra-virgin olive oil

> **Tip**
>
> Slice leftover chicken into strips and serve it over salad or in a wrap. You can also cube or shred it and make chicken salad.

Preheat the oven to 350°F. Lightly oil a baking dish just large enough to hold the chicken in a single layer.

Season the chicken with garlic powder, paprika, salt, and black pepper. Put a dollop of apricot preserves on each piece, and spread all over the chicken. Drizzle with a little olive oil. At this point, you can either bake the chicken, or cover and marinate it in the refrigerator for several hours or overnight.

Bake the chicken in the preheated oven, basting once or twice, until is cooked through, the juices run clear, and a meat thermometer inserted in the thickest part of the chicken reads at least 165°F, about 25 to 35 minutes, depending on size. About 10 minutes before they're done cooking, (or if the chicken starts to look dry), top the chicken pieces with additional preserves.

**STORAGE:** *Leftover chicken will keep well wrapped in the refrigerator for 2 to 3 days.*

# Arroz con Pollo

SERVES 4 TO 6 | MEAT

*When I asked the family about the dishes from my grandmothers that they remembered most, the responses skewed toward holiday favorites. I suppose the response bias makes sense, since everyone knew I was writing a kosher cookbook. So when I found the typewritten, laminated copy of this recipe, I was intrigued. It was one of the only detailed recipes in my grandmother's collection, which suggests she learned it from someone else and wanted to get it right. When I asked my mom if her mom ever made it, she replied, "Oh sure, all the time."*

*Prep time: 20 minutes*
*Cook time: 1 hour*

1 (3-pound) bone-in chicken, cut into 8 pieces

Sea salt or kosher salt

Freshly ground black pepper

2 tablespoons extra-virgin olive oil

1 large onion, peeled and chopped

3 garlic cloves, chopped

1 cup chopped red bell pepper

1 cup chopped green pepper

½ teaspoon loosely packed saffron threads

1 cup chopped, seeded tomatoes

½ cup dry white wine

½ cup long-grain white rice, such as basmati, rinsed

1 cup chicken or vegetable broth

2 sprigs fresh parsley

1 tablespoon freshly squeezed lemon juice

1 bay leaf

¼ teaspoon red pepper flakes

½ cup peas

1 or 2 jarred pimientos, or ¼ cup olives with pimientos, sliced

Season the chicken pieces with salt and pepper.

In a large Dutch oven or covered chef's pan, warm the oil over medium-high heat. Add the chicken pieces, skin-side down, and cook until golden, about 5 to 7 minutes. Turn and brown on the other side, about 4 to 6 minutes.

Scatter the onion, garlic, peppers, and saffron over the chicken. Stir the chicken pieces so that the vegetables and spices fall between them. Continue cooking until the vegetables begin to soften, about 3 to 5 minutes.

Stir in the tomatoes and wine. Add the rice and stir to distribute evenly around the chicken. Add the broth, parsley, lemon juice, bay leaf, red pepper flakes, and additional salt and pepper. Stir and cover with a tight-fitting lid. Bring to a boil, then reduce the heat and simmer for 40 minutes, or until the rice is tender and the chicken is cooked through, the juices run clear, and an instant-read thermometer inserted in the thickest part of a breast and thigh registers 165°F. *(CONTINUED)*

Just before the chicken finishes cooking, place the peas in a small saucepan with just enough water to cover. Bring to a boil, reduce the heat, and simmer until tender, about 5 to 8 minutes. Drain and set aside.

When the chicken is ready, garnish with the cooked peas and the pimientos or olives. Serve hot.

How-To

If you want the rice to have a soft, almost risotto-like texture, add it as instructed previously. If you prefer more distinctive grains and a soupier Arroz con Pollo, add all of the ingredients except the rice, and simmer for 20 to 25 minutes before adding the rice to the pot. After you add the rice, give the pot a stir, cover, and continue to simmer until the rice is tender and the chicken is cooked through.

# Persian Chicken Stew with Tomatoes and Green Beans

SERVES 4 TO 6 | MEAT

*I forget that were she still alive today, my grandmother would be a centenarian. In my mind, she never aged (or in her own, for that matter—every year on her birthday, she insisted she was 29+++). So sometimes, when I meet people who are about the age she was when she died, I'll have the strong sense they'd have been great friends if they'd had the chance to meet. My husband's best friend hails from a large Persian Jewish family, and whenever I see his mother, I can't help but think of my grandmother for precisely that reason. One evening, we were craving her excellent food, which I did my best to replicate. This khoresht loobia sabz, or Persian-style chicken stew with green beans, was the result.*

*Prep time: 20 minutes*
*Cook time: 1 hour, 20 minutes*

2 tablespoons extra-virgin olive oil

1 large onion, peeled, trimmed, and chopped

3 large garlic cloves, peeled and chopped

1½ pounds boneless, skinless chicken breasts, cut into ½-inch cubes

½ teaspoon cinnamon

½ teaspoon turmeric

¼ teaspoon ground cumin

1 (15-ounce) can whole peeled plum tomatoes, with juice

2½ cups water

1½ teaspoons kosher salt or sea salt

½ teaspoon coarsely ground black pepper

Generous pinch of saffron threads

Juice of 1 lime

1 pound green beans, trimmed and cut into 1-inch pieces

Warm the oil in a Dutch oven or stockpot. Add the onion and sauté for 5 to 7 minutes, or until soft and translucent. Add the garlic and sauté 1 minute more.

Add the chicken pieces to the onion and sprinkle with the cinnamon, turmeric, and cumin. Sauté until the chicken turns white on all sides, about 5 to 7 minutes.

Add the tomatoes and their juice to the pot, crushing them with your hands as you drop them in. Add the water, salt, and pepper. Crush the saffron between your fingers and add it to the pot. Stir in the lime juice. Bring to a boil, reduce the heat, and simmer, covered, for 45 minutes.

Add the green beans and simmer, partially covered, 15 to 20 minutes more, or until the chicken is cooked through and the beans are tender. Serve with rice.

IN THE KITCHEN WITH
# RONNIE FEIN

*"What's to be afraid of?" my grandma would often say to me in the kitchen. It's not that she was an adventurous cook. It's just that she didn't worry about the outcome. My grandma talked about adding a* bissel *of this or a* zhmenya *of that. To this day, I have no idea what* zhmenya *means, but I got the point. She wasn't afraid to add mushrooms to the potato strudel to see if it would turn out even better, or baste the turkey with pineapple juice rather than chicken stock. She always measured out ingredients with her hand instead of a cup. A recipe didn't need to be exact.*

*From her I learned to feel sure of myself, especially in the kitchen. I'll experiment with new methods and ingredients, never worried that something might not taste like the best food on earth. We are not running a restaurant. We are cooking for family and friends. This confidence she stirred in me is something that I now, as a grandma to five, want to pass on. I tell my grandchildren, "Cook. Enjoy yourself. Try new things. Don't worry if it isn't perfect."*

*Indeed, what's to be afraid of?*

RONNIE FEIN is a kosher cooking instructor and food writer. She is the author of the cookbooks *The Modern Kosher Kitchen* and *Hip Kosher*.

# Roasted Turkey Breast with Honey-Pineapple Glaze

MEAT
*Serves 4*
*Prep time: 10 minutes*
*Cook time: 1 hour, 15 minutes*

1½ cups pineapple juice

3 tablespoons honey

3 tablespoons apple cider vinegar

2 tablespoons soy sauce

1 tablespoon chopped fresh ginger

2 garlic cloves, chopped

½ teaspoon harissa

1 (3-pound) bone-in turkey breast half

Salt (optional)

**MIRI'S NOTE:** *When Ronnie shared this recipe with me, I was floored because it reminded me so much of something my grandmother would have adored. In fact, as I was going through her recipes, I found one for Pineapple-Orange Ginger Turkey. Ronnie's glaze—with its saucy reduction and hit of spicy harissa—is like a modern take on the Polynesian-inspired fare that my grandmother loved to entertain with when Tiki culture was having its heyday. Harissa, by the way, is a spicy chile-based condiment that hails from Tunisia, and is popular throughout North Africa and Israel. You can find it in Middle Eastern markets, and some supermarkets. If you can't track it down, try substituting sriracha.*

Preheat the oven to 400°F.

In a medium saucepan, combine the pineapple juice, honey, apple cider vinegar, soy sauce, ginger, garlic, and harissa. Whisk the ingredients until well blended. Bring to a boil over medium-high heat. Lower the heat and simmer for 10 to 12 minutes, or until thickened slightly and syrupy. Set aside to cool.

Rinse and dry the turkey breast and place it in a roasting pan. Sprinkle with salt, if using. Place the pan in the oven and immediately reduce the heat to 325°F.

Roast for 20 minutes. Pour half the juice mixture over the turkey. Continue to roast for another 20 minutes. Pour the remainder of the juice mixture over the turkey. Continue to roast the turkey for another 20 to 35 minutes, basting occasionally with the pan juices, until a meat thermometer placed in the thickest part of the breast measures 165°F.

Remove the turkey from the oven and let rest for about 15 minutes before carving. Serve with the pan drippings.

# Za'atar-Lemon Turkey Breast with Fennel

SERVES 4 TO 6 | MEAT

*I first tasted za'atar while wandering in the Old City in Jerusalem. I found myself in a quiet alley, where an old man stood selling* bageleh, *large, flattish, sesame-topped breads. I bought one, and he handed it to me with a little envelope of za'atar. I fell in love with the hyssop- and sumac-based spice blend. Now my daughter is similarly enraptured, so when I asked her what she thought I should put on our turkey she replied, "Za'atar. Za'atar belongs on everything!"*

*Prep time: 10 minutes*
*Cook time: 1 hour, 15 minutes*

3 large carrots, peeled and halved lengthwise

1 (2- to 2½-pound) boneless turkey breast

2 large fennel bulbs, trimmed and cut into wedges

2 large garlic cloves, finely chopped

2 tablespoons za'atar

Kosher salt or sea salt

Freshly ground black pepper

2 tablespoons extra-virgin olive oil

2 tablespoons freshly squeezed lemon juice

½ cup dry white wine

Preheat the oven to 425°F. In the center of a large roasting pan, arrange the carrots side by side, but not touching, to form a rack for the turkey. Lay the turkey breast, skin-side up, on top of the carrots. Place the fennel wedges around the perimeter of the pan, surrounding the turkey and carrots.

Loosen the turkey skin, and spread half the garlic and za'atar onto the meat underneath it. Spread the rest of the za'atar and garlic on the skin. Season with salt and a few turns of freshly ground pepper.

In a small bowl, whisk together the olive oil and lemon juice and pour evenly over the turkey breast. Pour the wine over the fennel.

Place the roasting pan in the oven and reduce the heat to 350°F. Roast for 40 minutes, baste with the pan juices, then roast for 20 minutes more. Check the temperature at the thickest part of the breast with an instant-read thermometer; when it registers 165°F, the turkey is done. If it is not yet ready, check in 15-minute increments to avoid overcooking.

When the turkey has finished cooking, remove from the oven, tent the pan with foil, and allow to rest for 10 minutes. Place on a carving board and slice, then transfer to a platter with the fennel and carrots. Drizzle with the pan juices and serve.

**STORAGE:** *Leftover turkey can be refrigerated for up to 4 days, or frozen for up to 3 months.*

# Pineapple Ginger Ribeyes

SERVES 4 TO 6 | MEAT

*My family has always had a thing for steak, whether as a celebratory meal or a casual treat. Despite my vegetarian leanings now, my parents have photos of me gleefully gnawing on steak bones cavegirl-style—proof that I, too, was an enthusiastic fan as a little kid. As an apartment dweller, my grandmother would broil them, but my parents were just as likely to throw steaks on the grill. I like to do the same, after marinating them in a tenderizing, zingy mix of pineapple juice, apple cider vinegar, garlic, and ginger.*

*Prep time: 15 minutes*
*Marinate time: 40 minutes, or overnight*
*Cook time: 10 minutes*

4 (10- to 12-ounce) boneless ribeye steaks

½ cup plus 2 tablespoons pineapple juice

2 tablespoons reduced-sodium soy sauce or tamari

2 tablespoons apple cider vinegar

1 tablespoon brown sugar

2 large garlic cloves, finely chopped

1½ teaspoons grated fresh ginger

Place the steaks in a nonreactive baking dish large enough to hold them in a single layer, or divide them between 2 gallon-size zipper-top freezer bags.

In a medium bowl, whisk together the pineapple juice, soy sauce, vinegar, brown sugar, garlic, and ginger. Pour over the steaks, and turn the meat to coat it on all sides. Cover the dish (or, if you are using zipper-top bags, squeeze out any air and seal), and refrigerate for a minimum of 40 minutes, or overnight.

To cook outdoors, oil the grate of a charcoal or gas grill and preheat until you have a hot fire. Remove the steaks from the marinade, and place on the grill. Discard any excess marinade. Grill the steaks to your preferred doneness. Depending on the thickness of the steaks, cooking time will vary, but allow about 5 minutes per side for a 1-inch to 1½-inch steak cooked to medium. If you prefer medium-well or well-done steaks, reduce the heat slightly after the initial sear so the outside does not burn while the inside cooks through. *(CONTINUED)*

To cook the steaks indoors, preheat the oven to 350°F. Place one or two cast iron grill pans over medium-high heat. Brush with oil, then add the steak. Sear for 2 minutes, flip, and sear for 2 minutes more on the other side. Transfer the skillet(s) to the oven and roast for about 4 minutes for medium. (If you have only one grill pan, work in batches and transfer both the steaks to a parchment-lined rimmed baking sheet to finish at the same time in the oven.)

Tip

Leftover steak tastes great in a salad. Slice the steak against the grain (see page 179 for a how-to). Serve over baby greens with steamed snap peas, cherry tomatoes, avocado, and corn. Add the slaw on page 84 for color and an automatic dressing.

# Wine-Braised Short Ribs with Kumquats

SERVES 4 TO 6 | MEAT

*Whenever she could get her hands on them, there were kumquats in my grandmother's fridge. I found everything about them fascinating, from their juxtaposed sweet and bitter flavors to the fact that the skin was actually edible. She never cooked with them, but when I set out to work on a short rib recipe, they immediately sprung to mind as the ideal accent for the rich, fall-off-the-bone meat.*

*Prep time: 15 minutes*
*Cook time: 3½ hours*

2 tablespoons canola or grapeseed oil

6 to 8 bone-in short ribs, 2½ to 4 inches long (about 4 pounds total)

Sea salt or kosher salt

Freshly ground black pepper

1 tablespoon Chinese five-spice powder or garam masala

1 large onion, sliced

2 carrots, peeled and cut into 1-inch pieces

2 celery stalks, cut into 1-inch pieces

8 to 10 garlic cloves, peeled and smashed

¼ cup Cointreau or triple sec

1 750-ml bottle dry red wine

1 pint kumquats, halved lengthwise, visible seeds removed

Preheat the oven to 325°F. Warm the oil in a Dutch oven set over medium-high heat. Season the ribs on all sides with the salt and pepper. Sprinkle with the five-spice powder or garam masala, and rub it into the meat. Working in batches if necessary, sear the ribs on all sides until browned, about 4 to 5 minutes per side.

If you worked in batches, return all of the ribs to the Dutch oven (you can place bone-in racks on their sides if they fit better). Add the onion, carrots, celery, and garlic to the pan. Lower the heat to medium, and sweat the vegetables, stirring once or twice, until the onions soften, about 5 minutes.

Pour the Cointreau over the ribs and cook for 2 minutes. Add the wine and kumquats, and bring to a boil. Cover the Dutch oven, and slide into the oven. Roast until very tender, turning occasionally if the ribs are long, about 2½ to 3 hours. *(CONTINUED)*

Use tongs to transfer the ribs to a serving platter and tent with foil to keep warm. Carefully skim as much fat as possible from the surface of the sauce. Place the Dutch oven over medium heat on the stove top and simmer for 10 minutes to reduce the sauce. Spoon some of the sauce over the ribs, along with the onions and kumquats. Serve immediately.

STORAGE: *Ribs can be made 1 to 2 days ahead and stored in their sauce, covered in the refrigerator. Spoon off any hardened fat from the surface of the sauce, then reheat them over low heat on the stove top.*

Tip

You can use individually cut short ribs, or racks of 3 to 4 ribs apiece (the racks tend to be less expensive). Either option is fine, as the ribs will practically fall off the bone once cooked.

# Classic Brisket with New Potatoes and Carrots

SERVES 6 TO 8 | MEAT

*Chances are good that if you've got a brisket-making bubbe in the family, her version looks a whole lot like this. Slow cooking transforms every ingredient: The meat becomes incredibly tender, the potatoes and carrots become soft and silky, and simple tomato paste and aromatics turn the juices into a rich gravy. This recipe uses a smaller brisket, so it is nice for occasions when you aren't feeding an army. My grandmother liked to use deckle, a more economical point cut with a little more fat (and flavor) than other roasts.*

*Prep time: 10 minutes*
*Cook time: 3½ hours*

1 large onion, peeled and chopped

4 carrots, peeled and cut into chunks

2 celery stalks, chopped

4 garlic cloves, smashed

1 (2- to 3-pound) brisket or deckle roast

Kosher salt or sea salt

Freshly ground black pepper

Garlic powder

1 (6-ounce) can tomato paste or 1 (15-ounce) can tomato sauce

1 pound baby potatoes

Preheat the oven to 350°F. Place the onion, carrots, celery, and garlic cloves in a roasting pan or large Dutch oven. Place the brisket on top of the vegetables. Season with salt, pepper, and garlic powder. Spread the tomato paste over the meat, then fill the can with water and add to the pan. (If you are using tomato sauce, pour it over the brisket but do not add extra water.) Toss a handful of the vegetables on top of the meat. Arrange the potatoes around the brisket.

Cover with foil or a lid. Cook in the preheated oven for 2 hours. Remove from the oven, uncover, and transfer the brisket to a cutting board. Trim the excess fat, then slice across the grain into slices ¼-inch thick or thinner. Place the brisket back in the pan, cover, and return to the oven for 1 to 1½ hours longer, or until the meat is fork tender.

### How-To

To feed a crowd, you can roast two 2- to 3-pound roasts side by side in a large roasting pan, or opt for a larger brisket. Just double the vegetables, tomato sauce, and potatoes.

# Cranberry Horseradish Brisket

SERVES 8 TO 10 | MEAT

*The title on the recipe card read "Brisket Shel Yerushalaim," meaning "Brisket of Jerusalem." The simple instructions were capped with the comment, "As Yerushalaim is sweeter each time you return, this roast is better when reheated the next day!" I was instantly charmed. Putting aside that cranberries aren't remotely indigenous to Israel, I was intrigued by the short ingredient list of cranberry sauce, horseradish, and a little cinnamon; would this recipe be absolutely delicious, or sort of odd? I opted for homemade cranberry sauce instead of jellied, and added wine, just because. I'm happy to report that even the day it was made, it drew raves.*

*Prep time: 15 minutes*
*Cook time: 4 ½ hours*

12 ounces fresh or frozen cranberries

1 cup water

½ cup plus 2 tablespoons sugar

¼ cup honey

½ cup prepared white horseradish

1 cup dry red wine

½ cup water or beef stock

3 tablespoons tamari soy sauce

½ teaspoon cinnamon

2 tablespoons extra-virgin olive oil or canola oil

1 (4 ½- to 5-pound) brisket, first or second cut

Preheat the oven to 325°F. In a medium saucepan, combine the cranberries, water, sugar, and honey and bring to a boil. Reduce the heat and simmer uncovered for 10 to 15 minutes, stirring occasionally, until the sauce begins to thicken. Stir in the horseradish, wine, water or stock, tamari, and cinnamon. Return to a boil, reduce the heat, and simmer for 10 minutes to reduce slightly. Remove from the heat.

Place a stovetop-safe roasting pan over medium-high heat. Warm the oil, then add the brisket, and sear until nicely browned, about 7 to 8 minutes. Carefully turn the meat and sear the other side, about 5 to 7 minutes more. Pour the cranberry mixture over the meat.

Cover the roasting pan with a lid or foil, tenting it if necessary so that it does not touch the meat. Cook in the preheated oven for 2 hours.

Remove the roasting pan from the oven, uncover, and carefully transfer the brisket to a cutting board. With a large, sharp knife, cut across the grain into slices no more than ¼-inch thick. Transfer the sliced brisket back to the roasting pan as you work, laying the slices in the sauce.

Cover the pan and continue roasting for 1½ to 2 hours more, or until the meat is fall-apart tender. To serve, carefully transfer the brisket to a serving platter and drizzle with some of the pan juices.

STORAGE: *Store the brisket and pan sauces in separate containers in the refrigerator for up to 2 days or in the freezer for up to 3 months.*

*Before reheating, remove any hardened fat from the surface of the sauce, and trim the brisket of excess fat. Preheat the oven to 350°F. Place the brisket and some of the sauce in a baking dish, cover, and cook for about 40 minutes, or until the brisket is hot.*

### How-To

One of the tricks to ensuring a tender brisket is to slice it properly. Take a look at the direction of the meat's grain—the long muscle fibers that run alongside each other. Hold a large, sharp knife at a slight angle, perpendicular to the grain, and slice. This is slicing across the grain, or against the grain.

# Cloak and Dagger

SERVES 2 HUNGRY PEOPLE OR 4 GOOD SHARERS  |  MEAT

*Until I tried to research it, I didn't realize that the Cloak and Dagger is little known out-side of Baltimore. Attman's, a Jewish deli and Charm City fixture since 1915, claims to have originated the sandwich, which may be a kosher-style answer to the Reuben. (Though the deli wasn't kosher, the menu originally eschewed blatantly non-kosher combos.) My grandparents would head to the Knish Shop, a local kosher deli, for sand-wich fixings, rye bread, pickles, and salads, and we'd assemble our favorites around the kitchen table. I adored the spy novel mysteriousness of the name Cloak and Dagger as much as I loved the corned beef, coleslaw, and Russian dressing combo.*

*Prep time: 5 minutes*

FOR THE RUSSIAN DRESSING

2 tablespoons mayonnaise

2 tablespoons ketchup

1 teaspoon prepared white horseradish

1 teaspoon finely chopped pickles (optional)

FOR THE SANDWICHES

8 ounces corned beef

4 slices rye or marble rye bread

1 cup coleslaw, store-bought or homemade

Simple Swap

Don't have pickles? Chopped capers make a tasty, if nontraditional, addition to the dressing.

MAKE THE DRESSING: In a small bowl, mix together the mayonnaise, ketchup, horseradish, and pickles (if using).

MAKE THE SANDWICHES: Divide the corned beef between 2 slices of rye bread. Top with ½ cup of coleslaw, and spread to cover the corned beef. Generously spread 2 more slices of rye bread with Russian dressing, and place, dressing side down, on top of the sandwiches. Slice each sandwich in half and serve immedi-ately, preferably with a dill pickle on the side.

Kasha Varnishkes with Ratatouille (page 184)

# CHAPTER NINE

# Meatless Mains

I started eating mostly vegetarian when I landed in a studio apartment with a little galley kitchen. It was just easier to deal with a single set of dishes and cookware than to try to find storage space for meat, dairy, and pareve kitchenware. Plus, without the expense of meat, I could afford whatever caught my eye at the farmers' market, or to splurge on organic produce, tropical fruits, and unusual grains. My grandmothers, who contended with wartime rationing, would probably have understood the drive to find creative, economical ways to pull good meals together without meat at their center. And they certainly appreciated the appeal of a good dairy (if not vegan) meal. But what I love most about vegetarian dishes is that so many world cuisines include them, and they're the most obvious starting point for kosher keepers to explore the flavors of other countries.

# Kasha Varnishkes with Ratatouille

SERVES 4 TO 6 | PAREVE

*For my forebears, kasha varnishkes, or toasted buckwheat groats with bowtie pasta and onions, was a humble, though much loved, side dish. But for me, it's an ideal meal, topped with oven-roasted ratatouille, rich with eggplant, peppers, tomato, zucchini, and a hefty dose of basil. It's still pure comfort food, but it's painted in broader, more colorful brushstrokes, and to my eye—and palate—the picture feels more complete. Crumbled goat cheese or feta adds even more delicious dimension to this dish, if you want to make it dairy.*

*Prep time: 25 minutes*
*Cook time: 45 minutes*

## FOR THE RATATOUILLE

3 tablespoons extra-virgin olive oil

1 large onion, peeled and chopped

3 large garlic cloves, chopped

1 medium eggplant, cut into 1-inch pieces

1 large red bell pepper, cored and chopped

1 medium zucchini, trimmed and cut into
 1-inch pieces

2 medium tomatoes, seeded and cut into
 1-inch pieces

2 tablespoons tomato paste or tomato sauce

Generous pinch dried thyme

2 tablespoons thinly sliced fresh basil leaves,
 plus extra for garnish

Sea salt or kosher salt

Freshly ground black pepper

## FOR THE KASHA VARNISHKES

4 tablespoons extra-virgin olive oil or canola
 oil, divided

1 large onion, peeled and finely chopped

1 pound bowtie (farfalle) noodles

1 large egg

1 cup kasha (medium granulation)

2 cups water or vegetable stock

1 teaspoon salt

¼ teaspoon freshly ground black pepper

### Simple Swap

If you can't find granulated kasha, whole kasha works too (pictured on page 182). It will take least 15 to 20 minutes to cook, but the rest of the method remains the same.

**MAKE THE RATATOUILLE:** Preheat the oven to 400°F. Warm the oil in a Dutch oven or ovenproof covered chef's pan set over medium heat. Add the chopped onion and sauté until it softens and begins to turn translucent, about 5 minutes. Add the garlic and sauté 1 minute more.

Add the chopped eggplant and cook, stirring frequently, until it begins to soften, about 5 minutes. Add the red peppers, sauté for 2 minutes, then add the zucchini, stirring occasionally, until the zucchini softens, about 3 minutes more. Stir in the tomatoes, tomato paste (or sauce) and thyme.

Cover the pan and place in the preheated oven. Bake for 30 minutes, stirring after 15 minutes. The vegetables should be saucy and tender, yet still mostly hold their shape. Remove from the oven, stir in the basil, and season with salt and pepper. Set aside.

**MAKE THE KASHA VARNISHKES:** While the ratatouille is baking, set a large pot of water to boil for the pasta. In a chef's pan or large skillet, heat 2 tablespoons of oil over medium-high heat. Add the onions and sauté until they turn soft and translucent, about 5 minutes. Reduce the heat and cook, stirring occasionally, until the onions start to caramelize, about 10 minutes more. Remove from the heat and set aside.

In the meantime, when the pasta water comes to a boil, stir in the bowties and cook until al dente, about 10 to 11 minutes. Drain and transfer the pasta to a large serving bowl.

In a small bowl, beat the egg. Add the kasha and stir well to coat the kasha grains. Transfer the onions from the chef's pan to the serving bowl with the pasta. Return the pan to the stove top and place over medium heat. Add the kasha and cook, stirring constantly, until the egg dries and the kasha separates into individual grains, about 3 minutes.

Add the water or stock to the kasha and bring to a boil. Reduce the heat, cover, and simmer until the liquid is absorbed, about 10 minutes.

When the kasha is cooked, add to the bowl with the bowties and onion. Drizzle with 2 tablespoons of oil and stir well to combine. Spoon into shallow bowls and top with the ratatouille. Garnish with additional basil.

**STORAGE:** *Store the ratatouille and the kasha varnishkes in separate covered containers in the refrigerator. The ratatouille will keep for 4 to 5 days, the kasha for 2 to 3 days. You can also freeze both dishes in freezer-safe containers for up to 3 months.*

# Savory Vegetable Pot Pie

SERVES 4 TO 6 | DAIRY OR PAREVE

*When I was a kid, I was fascinated by the cornucopia that was the supermarket freezer aisle. Because there were relatively few kosher options, I thought they were all exciting—especially the chicken pot pies, with their puff pastry lids. Nowadays, I'd much rather have this homemade vegetarian take on the American classic, rich with wine-braised veggies and flaky, butter-rich pastry.*

*Prep time: 25 minutes*
*Cook time: 50 minutes*

1½ pounds butternut squash, peeled, seeded, and cut into ½-inch cubes (about 3½ cups)

1 tablespoon extra-virgin olive oil

2 tablespoons unsalted butter (or olive oil if pareve)

½ small red onion, peeled and finely chopped

3 large garlic cloves, chopped

10 ounces cremini mushrooms, cleaned, trimmed; quartered if small, cut into wedges if large

½ cup dry white wine

2 tablespoons all-purpose flour

2 cups vegetable stock

8 ounces cauliflower, broken into small florets (about 1½ cups)

12 to 14 spears asparagus, trimmed and cut into ½-inch pieces (about 1 cup)

½ cup fresh or frozen peas

Leaves from 1 sprig fresh oregano, chopped (or ¼ teaspoon dried)

Sea salt or kosher salt

Freshly ground black pepper

1 sheet (from a 14- to 17-ounce package) all-butter or pareve puff pastry, thawed if frozen

Preheat the oven to 425°F. Place the squash cubes in a single layer on a rimmed baking sheet or in a roasting pan, drizzle with olive oil, and toss to coat. Roast in the preheated oven, stirring once or twice, until the squash is tender, about 20 to 25 minutes. Remove from the oven, then lower the heat to 400°F.

In the meantime, set a large chef's pan or Dutch oven over medium-high heat. Add the butter and melt (or warm the olive oil). Add the onion and sauté until soft and translucent, 5 to 7 minutes. Stir in the garlic and mushrooms. Sauté for 5 minutes, or until the mushrooms soften and release their juices. Add the wine. Stirring frequently, continue to cook until most of the liquid in the pan has cooked off, about 3 minutes more.

Sprinkle the mushrooms evenly with the flour and toss to coat. Add the stock and cauliflower florets, stirring until the sauce begins to thicken. Stir in the asparagus and peas. Simmer gently for 8 to 10 minutes, or until the vegetables are tender. Add the cooked squash, folding to combine. Season with the oregano, salt, and pepper.

Transfer the vegetables to a 2- or 3-quart baking dish or individual ovenproof ramekins or crocks. Top with the puff pastry, trimming with a sharp knife to fit. Cut a few 1-inch slits through the crust. Bake 30 to 35 minutes, or until the pastry is puffed and golden brown. Allow to rest for 5 to 10 minutes before serving—the filling will be hot!

# Forbidden Rice Bowl with Tofu, Sweet Potato, and Greens

SERVES 4 | PAREVE

*This first time I made this, I was just trying to get dinner on the table, throwing things together I was pretty sure my kids could be relied upon to eat. Then my daughter, who had appointed herself arbiter of which recipes were "book good," gave it an enthusiastic thumbs-up, while her little brother gobbled away. The colorful combo of black rice (which looks purple when cooked), roasted tofu, and sweet potatoes, topped with sautéed greens, has become a go-to on busy nights, especially ever since I hit on the tahini-miso drizzle that ties it all together.*

*Prep time: 20 minutes*
*Cook time: 40 minutes*

### FOR THE RICE, TOFU, AND VEGETABLES

1 cup forbidden (black) rice

1¾ cups water

1 (16-ounce package) extra-firm tofu, drained

1 black tea bag, such as English breakfast, oolong, or Darjeeling

¼ cup boiling water

¼ cup pure maple syrup (dark)

2 tablespoons tamari soy sauce

1 tablespoon rice vinegar

1 teaspoon toasted sesame oil

¼ teaspoon cinnamon

⅛ teaspoon garam masala

1¼ pounds sweet potatoes or garnet yams, peeled and cut into ½-inch cubes

2 tablespoons extra-virgin olive oil, divided

2 garlic cloves, chopped or thinly sliced

1 pound baby spinach, kale, tatsoi, or a mix, rinsed but not dried

### FOR THE MISO-TAHINI SAUCE

¼ to ½ cup warm water

¼ cup white or yellow miso

¼ cup tahini (sesame paste)

1 tablespoon rice vinegar

1 to 2 tablespoons pure maple syrup

### Simple Swap

If you don't have tofu—or just want to cut down on the prep time—you can skip it and top the bowls with boiled, shelled edamame (soy beans).

MAKE THE RICE: Preheat the oven to 425°F. Combine the rice and water in a saucepan. Bring to a boil, reduce the heat, and simmer, covered, for 30 to 35 minutes, or until the rice is nearly tender and the water is absorbed. Allow to sit, covered, for 5 to 10 minutes more.

MAKE THE TOFU AND VEGETABLES: Line a cutting board or baking sheet with a few layers of paper towels. Cut the tofu crosswise into ¾-inch slices and lay them flat on the paper towels. Top with another layer of towels and press down gently to remove as much water as you can from the tofu. Remove the top layer of towels, and cut the tofu slices into cubes.

Place the teabag in a heat-proof bowl and pour the boiling water over it. Let it steep for 2 minutes, then remove and discard the teabag. Add the maple syrup, tamari, rice vinegar, sesame oil, cinnamon, and garam masala to the water, and whisk well. Add the tofu to the bowl and toss gently to coat. Pour the tofu and marinade into a baking dish or rimmed baking sheet large enough to hold it in a single layer.

Place the cubed sweet potatoes on a rimmed baking sheet. Drizzle with 1 tablespoon of olive oil and toss to coat. Put the tofu and sweet potatoes into the preheated oven. Roast for about 20 to 25 minutes, turning the tofu and potatoes a couple of times during cooking, or until the tofu is firm and the sweet potatoes are tender and beginning to caramelize.

In a large chef's pan, wok, or wide, deep skillet, warm 1 tablespoon of olive oil over medium-high heat. Add the garlic and sauté for 1 minute. Add the greens with any water still clinging to the leaves. Toss until the greens wilt, about 2 to 3 minutes. Remove from the heat and set aside.

MAKE THE MISO-TAHINI SAUCE: In a small bowl, whisk together ¼ cup warm water, miso, tahini, rice vinegar, and 1 tablespoon maple syrup. Taste and adjust with additional water and/or maple syrup for a thinner and/or sweeter sauce.

To serve, divide the rice among 4 bowls. Top the rice with sweet potatoes, tofu, and greens. Drizzle each rice bowl with a little tahini-miso sauce, and serve the rest on the side.

# Roasted Beet Reuben

SERVES 2 | DAIRY

*I'm not sure how I went from being a despiser of beets to the sort of person who will put them on a sandwich. Maybe I'm turning into my grandmother. If a beet sandwich strikes you as weird, consider that when I first hit on this combo, I actually baked rye bread every few days for 2 weeks straight, just so I could eat it for lunch nearly every day.*

*Prep time: 10 minutes*
*Cook time: 50 minutes*

2 small beets, greens removed and trimmed

Extra-virgin olive oil

¼ cup mayonnaise

1 small garlic clove, finely chopped

1 teaspoon finely grated ginger

1 teaspoon freshly squeezed lemon juice

Pinch of sea salt or kosher salt

4 slices Homemade Seeded Rye Bread
   (page 231) or storebought

2 to 4 slices Swiss cheese

½ cup sauerkraut, drained

1 small apple, cored and thinly sliced

1 teaspoon extra-virgin olive oil

1 teaspoon butter

Preheat the oven to 425°F. Rub the beets with a little olive oil, wrap in foil, and place in a baking pan. Slide into the oven and roast for 35 to 40 minutes, or until the beets are tender. When the beets are cool enough to handle, peel and slice into ¼-inch rounds. Set aside.

In a small bowl, whisk together the mayonnaise, garlic, ginger, lemon juice, and salt. Cover and refrigerate.

To assemble the sandwiches: Spread 2 slices of rye bread with the mayonnaise spread. Top with Swiss cheese, ¼ cup sauerkraut, a layer of apple slices, and a layer of beet slices. Top with a second slice of bread, spread with more ginger mayonnaise if you'd like. Repeat with the second sandwich.

In a cast iron or other heavy skillet set over medium-high heat, warm the olive oil and butter. When the butter melts and begins to foam, carefully add the sandwiches, cheese side closest to the pan. Press down with the back of a flat spatula. Cook for 3 to 4 minutes per side, or until the cheese melts, the sandwich is warmed through, and the bread is toasty and golden brown.

# Vegetarian Paella

SERVES 4 TO 6 | PAREVE

*This recipe reminds me a bit of my grandmother's Arroz con Pollo (page 167), sans chicken of course. I imagine she'd have loved this, too, had Arborio rice or kale been on her radar. Saffron and artichokes would have certainly piqued her interest, as would the kosher take on a Spanish cuisine classic.*

*Prep time: 15 minutes*
*Cook time: 25 minutes*

---

½ cup water

½ teaspoon saffron threads

2 tablespoons extra-virgin olive oil

1 medium onion, chopped

1 large carrot, peeled, halved lengthwise, and sliced

¾ cup frozen artichoke hearts or bottoms

2 large garlic cloves, finely chopped

1½ cups Arborio rice

¾ teaspoon paprika

¾ teaspoon sea salt

3 cups vegetable stock

1 medium bunch purple or green kale, tough center stems removed, leaves finely chopped (about 2 cups)

1 cup chopped tomatoes

1 cup fresh or frozen peas

1 lemon, cut into wedges

### Simple Swap

If artichokes are a kashrut concern in your community, you can leave them out of the recipe, and add bell peppers or asparagus instead.

In a small saucepan set over medium-high heat, bring ½ cup water to a boil. Crumble in the saffron and remove the pot from the heat.

In a large chef's pan, paella pan, or wok set over medium-high heat, warm the olive oil. Add the chopped onion and carrot. Sauté until the onions begin to soften and turn translucent, about 5 to 7 minutes. Add the artichoke hearts or bottoms and sauté for about 3 minutes, until the artichokes are heated through and start to soften. Add the garlic and sauté until fragrant, about 1 minute more.

Add the rice and sauté until it is coated with oil and starts to turn translucent, about 1 to 2 minutes. Add the saffron water, paprika, and sea salt, and coat the rice with the spices. Pour in the vegetable stock. Stir in the chopped kale and tomatoes, and bring to a boil. Reduce the heat to medium-low, cover, and simmer for 15 minutes, until most of the liquid is absorbed.

Add the peas. Stir well, cover, and simmer for about 5 minutes, or until the rice is tender. Remove from the heat and let stand, covered, for 5 minutes more. Spoon the paella into shallow bowls, and serve with lemon wedges on the side.

# Corn and Spinach Quesadillas with Saucy Black Beans

SERVES 4 | DAIRY

*When I think about my grandmother's cooking, I usually think of elaborate meals. But the reality is that there were plenty of times she needed to get a meal on the table quickly. She opted for DIY deli sandwiches, egg salad, or tuna. When my kids are hungry NOW and I need a go-to meal I can make on autopilot, it's often these quesadillas.*

*Prep time: 15 minutes*
*Cook time: 15 minutes*

### FOR THE BEANS

1 (15-ounce) can black beans, drained and rinsed

½ cup water

2 tablespoons tamari soy sauce

1 tablespoon balsamic vinegar

### FOR THE QUESADILLAS

1 tablespoon extra-virgin olive oil, plus more for the pan

10 ounces frozen chopped spinach

1 cup frozen corn kernels

8 whole-wheat tortillas

1 cup shredded Cheddar cheese

½ cup shredded mozzarella cheese

½ cup goat cheese crumbles (optional)

### TO SERVE

Salsa

Avocado (chopped or sliced), or guacamole

Sour cream

Hot sauce

**MAKE THE BEANS:** In a small saucepan, combine the beans, water, tamari, and vinegar. Bring to a boil, reduce the heat, and simmer, uncovered, until the liquid reduces and the beans turn saucy, about 8 to 10 minutes. Remove from the heat and set aside.

**MAKE THE QUESADILLAS:** In a large skillet (cast iron is ideal) set over medium-high heat, warm the oil. Add the spinach and corn and sauté until the vegetables are cooked through and any water in the pan evaporates, about 5 to 7 minutes. Transfer to a bowl.

Wipe out the skillet. Add a little olive oil. Place a tortilla in the skillet, top with ¼ of the Cheddar and ¼ of the mozzarella. Crumble on goat cheese, if using. Spoon on ¼ of the spinach and corn mixture and spread evenly over the cheese. Top with a second tortilla and cook over medium heat, flipping once, until the cheese is melted, about 2 minutes per side. Transfer to a plate and repeat with the remaining ingredients. As each quesadilla leaves the pan, stack it on the others to keep them warm.

When all of the quesadillas are cooked, cut into wedges and serve with salsa, avocado, sour cream, and/or hot sauce.

# Basil Pesto and Pea Pasta

SERVES 4 AS A MAIN DISH, OR 6 TO 8 AS A FIRST COURSE | DAIRY OR PAREVE

*Like many cooks of her generation, my grandmother relied on the contents of a well-stocked spice cabinet to season her dishes. Growing up, I was fascinated by her collection of dried basil, oregano, marjoram, bay leaves, chives, dill, rosemary, and so many more, and by her knowledge of when to use what. But she also insisted on fresh parsley for recipes as important as her matzo balls. I'm positive that had fresh basil been as readily available, she'd have embraced pesto-making as well.*

*Prep time: 30 minutes*
*Cook time: 12 minutes*

2 ¼ cups packed fresh basil leaves, rinsed well and patted dry

½ cup toasted pine nuts

2 large garlic cloves, chopped

⅓ to ½ cup extra-virgin olive oil, plus extra for drizzling

⅔ cup freshly grated Parmesan cheese, preferably Parmigiano-Reggiano (optional)

Sea salt or kosher salt

2 cups fresh or frozen peas

1 pound pasta, such as farfalle, orecchiette, bucatini, or spaghetti

Bring a large pot and a medium saucepan of water to a boil on separate burners.

In the work bowl of a food processor fitted with an S blade, place the basil, pine nuts, and garlic. Pulse several times to make a coarsely chopped paste. Slowly add ⅓ cup of the olive oil while pulsing a few more times, until the oil is integrated and the pesto is fairly smooth, but still has some texture.

If you're using the cheese and have a dairy food processor, add it to the work bowl and pulse a few times. Otherwise, transfer the pesto to a bowl and stir in the grated Parmesan. Drizzle in more olive oil if you prefer a thinner pesto. If you're not using cheese, taste the pesto and season with sea salt or kosher salt. Cover and refrigerate until ready to use.

When the large pot of water reaches a rapid boil, stir in the pasta. Cook according to package directions until al dente, then drain and transfer to a large bowl or serving platter. Drizzle with a little olive oil and toss to coat.

In the meantime, when the medium saucepan reaches a boil, add the peas and cook until tender, about 2 to 3 minutes for fresh or 4 to 5 minutes for frozen. Drain the peas and set aside.

When the peas have finished cooking, add them, along with about ¾ of the pesto, to the cooked pasta. Gently toss together with two large serving spoons, so the pasta and peas are coated with pesto. Serve immediately with the extra pesto on the side, if desired.

Did You Know?

When the world's only producer of kosher Parmigiano-Reggiano ceased production several years ago, kosher–observant cheese lovers mourned the loss. But in late 2015, at least two Italian cheesemakers stepped in to fill the void. If you can't find it, try Grana Padano or Pecorino Romano.

# Spinach and Ricotta Manicotti

SERVES 6 TO 8 | DAIRY

*Since both my mother and grandmother made manicotti (or sometimes shells) stuffed with cheese, I thought of the dish as a family recipe and didn't really associate it with Italian-American cuisine. Of course, I knew better by the time I got the recipe at my wedding shower from a family friend of Italian extraction. It's virtually the same recipe I later dug up in my grandmother's collection—proving there's something to the joking assertions that Jewish and Italian grandmothers are cut from the same cloth. If you need convincing, check out the story from my old boss, Mitchell Davis, and his Jewish Spaghetti recipe (which follows this one).*

*Prep time: 30 minutes*
*Cook time: 50 minutes*

1 tablespoon extra-virgin olive oil

1 large garlic clove, chopped

1 (16-ounce) package frozen chopped spinach

1 pound dry manicotti shells

2 (15- to 16-ounce) packages ricotta cheese

1 (8 ounce) mozzarella cheese, grated

2 large eggs, lightly beaten

2 tablespoons chopped fresh basil

½ cup finely grated Parmesan cheese, preferably Parmigiano-Reggiano, divided

4 cups marinara sauce (jarred or homemade)

Preheat the oven to 350°F. Line a rimmed baking sheet with parchment or wax paper.

In a chef's pan or a large, deep skillet, warm the olive oil over medium-high heat. Add the garlic and spinach. Sauté until the spinach thaws and cooks through, about 5 to 7 minutes. Remove from the heat and transfer to a large bowl.

Bring a large pot of water to a boil. Add the manicotti shells and cook according to package directions until al dente, about 7 to 8 minutes. Drain and place on the parchment-lined baking sheet. (Make sure they are not touching one another, or they will stick together.)

To the bowl with the spinach, add the ricotta, mozzarella, eggs, basil, and ¼ cup of the Parmesan. Mix well.

Spread about 1 cup of sauce over the bottom of a 13-by-9-by- 2-inch baking pan. Fill a pastry bag (without a tip) with the cheese mixture, and use it to fill the manicotti shells from both ends, placing them in a single layer in the baking pan as you work.

Pour the rest of the sauce over the manicotti and sprinkle evenly with the remaining Parmesan. Bake, uncovered, in the preheated oven until bubbly, about 30 to 35 minutes.

How-To

If you don't have a pastry bag, you can use a zipper-top bag. Put the cheese mixture in the bag, gather the top and twist it closed, and snip off a small piece of the bag's bottom corner. Squeeze out the filling through the hole in the bottom.

## IN THE KITCHEN WITH
# MITCHELL DAVIS

*Learning there was no such thing as Jewish spaghetti—or rather, that no one outside of my family had ever heard of it—was a blow to my culinary innocence, right up there with the revelation that food stylists used inedible tricks in photos and Twinkies weren't baked. The soft noodles tossed in a sweet, buttery tomato sauce that we called Jewish Spaghetti appeared regularly alongside matzo meal-breaded fillets of sole and other main courses in the Davis dinner rotation. My mother learned to make it from her grandmother, Eva Knaster, the familial food legend, whose delicate touch in the kitchen all the Knaster women, and a few men, have since tried in vain to channel. (Her baked rice custard pudding remains but a memory.)*

*Four of Eva's eight children were daughters, including my grandmother, Rose, and all of them and their daughters could make an acceptable recreation of Eva's Jewish Spaghetti. That's a lot of family. No doubt there's a culinary node in Bergen County, New Jersey, where Jewish Spaghetti forms a subset of the local cuisine.*

*By the time I was in elementary school, we were living in north Toronto. For an innocent fifth-grade assignment we were asked to talk about our favorite food. I picked what I assumed to be a common dish and described my love of Jewish Spaghetti. I was met by blank stares, I assumed because of the high proportion of goyim in the group. The Jews were equally clueless, of course.*

*Any small pasta will do, though elbow macaroni is traditional in my family. Left to sit, the cooked noodles absorb the sauce—a combination of plain tomato sauce (no herbs or other Italian seasoning), a copious amount of butter, a little sugar to adjust the sweetness of the tomatoes, and salt—making them comfortingly soft, like a good mac 'n' cheese.*

*Years ago, while working in the kitchen of a restaurant in Turin, Italy, I was struck one night by the staff meal. Our chef, Luigi, prepared a simple spaghetti al pomodoro, the sauce a purée of partially dried Neapolitan tomatoes that had a concentrated sweetness and tomato paste flavor. Finished with butter and grated Parmesan cheese, the dish bore a striking resemblance to the Jewish Spaghetti of my childhood—enough to make me wonder if Jewish Spaghetti had really been Italian all along.*

**MITCHELL DAVIS** is the author of several cookbooks, including *The Mensch Chef* (from which this recipe is adapted), and the executive vice president of the James Beard Foundation.

# Jewish Spaghetti

DAIRY
*Serves 6 to 8*
*Prep time: 15 minutes*
*Cook time: 20 minutes*

1 pound elbow macaroni or similar
    small pasta

½ cup (1 stick) unsalted butter

2¼ cups plain tomato sauce, such
    as Hunt's

2 to 3 tablespoons sugar

½ teaspoon kosher salt, plus more for
    the cooking water

Freshly ground black pepper

**NOTE:** *To reheat after the dish has sat, there are two options. Either transfer the pasta to a 2-quart baking dish. Dot the top with a tablespoon or so of butter, cover with foil, and bake in a preheated 350°F oven for about 30 minutes. Remove the cover and bake a few more minutes until crisp on top. Or just reheat on top of the stove over low heat, stirring frequently to prevent burning.*

Bring a large pot of salted water to a boil. Add the pasta, stir, and cook until just past al dente, about 9 minutes. Drain, but do not rinse.

Meanwhile, in a medium saucepan melt the butter over medium-low heat. Add the tomato sauce, 4 tablespoons of sugar, salt, and season with pepper. The amount of sugar necessary will depend on the sweetness of the tomato sauce. Use just enough sugar to remove any bitter flavor and give a sweet tomato taste. It should not be candy sweet.

Add the drained noodles to the sauce and stir to coat. Turn off the heat, cover, and if you have time, let sit several hours at room temperature so the noodles absorb the sauce. If you don't have the time to let it sit, keep the heat on low and cook the pasta, stirring frequently, for 4 or 5 minutes until there's no liquid sauce evident.

# White Bean Cassoulet

SERVES 4 TO 6 | PAREVE

*Neither Bubbe nor my grandmother were cholent people. They didn't care for the slow-cooked bean- and meat-rich Shabbat stew, traditionally left in an oven Friday night so that there would be hot food for lunch the next day. They didn't make it, and probably as a result, no one in the family developed a taste for it. But I do love beans, and when root vegetables replace flanken and kishke, we're talking my kind of Shabbat or holiday lunch. Though the slow simmer yields the most flavorful beans, you can use 2 cans of beans, drained, in place of dry, and simmer for just about 30 minutes.*

*Prep time: 20 minutes*
*Cook time: 1 hour, 30 minutes*
*Soaking time: 1 hour*

### FOR THE CASSOULET

1 cup great northern beans, picked over
    and rinsed
6 cups water
3 tablespoons extra-virgin olive oil
1 large onion, peeled and chopped into
    ¼-inch dice
3 carrots, peeled, and cut into chunks
4 large garlic cloves, chopped
3½ cups vegetable stock
½ cup water
1 rutabaga, peeled and cut into 1-inch pieces
1 turnip, peeled and cut into 1-inch pieces
1 celery root, peeled and cut into 1-inch pieces
1 large tomato, seeded and chopped
1 tablespoon tomato paste or sauce
2 teaspoons dried thyme
¼ cup dry white wine

### FOR THE TOPPING

1 cup bread crumbs
2 tablespoons extra-virgin olive oil
3 large garlic cloves, chopped

**MAKE THE BEANS:** In a large saucepan, combine the beans and water. Bring to a rapid boil for 2 minutes, then remove from the heat, cover, and allow to soak for 1 hour. Drain and rinse the beans.

In a Dutch oven or large chef's pan set over medium-high heat, warm the oil. Add the onion, carrots, and garlic and cook, stirring frequently, until the onions are soft and translucent, about 5 to 7 minutes.

Add the beans, stock, water, rutabaga, turnip, celery root, tomato, tomato paste, and thyme. Bring to a boil, reduce the heat, and simmer, covered, for 45 minutes. Stir in the wine and simmer 15 to 45 minutes more, or until the beans are tender.

**MAKE THE TOPPING:** Preheat the oven to 400°F. In a small bowl, toss together the bread crumbs, olive oil, and garlic. Sprinkle evenly over the cassoulet, and bake, uncovered, for 10 to 15 minutes, or until the bread crumbs are crisp and golden.

# Matzo Spanakopita

SERVES 6 TO 8 | DAIRY

*I'm one of those people who actually likes matzo. But about midway through Passover, I want to find something fresh to do with it, without trying to turn it into something it's not. With Sephardic minas (matzo pies) on my mind, I realized it would make a great stand-in for filo dough (and require none of the careful handling of those paper-thin sheets). Now we enjoy spanakopita for Passover—and months later, too, when I discover there's still some matzo left over in the pantry.*

*Prep time: 15 minutes*
*Cook time: 1 hour*

2 tablespoons extra-virgin olive oil, plus extra for drizzling

1 large onion, chopped

1 pound baby spinach or mixed baby greens (such as chard, mustard greens, or kale), rinsed but not dried

2 medium zucchini, trimmed and coarsely shredded

1 pound sheep's or cow's milk feta cheese

¼ to ⅓ cup chopped fresh dill

Pinch of nutmeg

Freshly ground black pepper

4 sheets matzo

Preheat the oven to 375°F. Oil a 9-by-13-by-2-inch glass baking dish.

In a chef's pan or large, deep skillet, warm the olive oil over medium-high heat. Add the onion and sauté until soft and translucent, about 5 to 7 minutes. Add the spinach (or greens) to the pan and sauté until the leaves wilt, release their water, and the liquid in the pan cooks off, about 5 minutes more. Transfer the spinach mixture to a large bowl.

Using paper towels or a clean tea towel, squeeze as much liquid as you can from the zucchini. Add a little more olive oil to the pan if needed, and add the zucchini. Sauté until the zucchini cooks through, releases its water, and any liquid in the pan cooks off. Add to the bowl with the spinach, and toss together.

Crumble the feta into the vegetable mixture and mix well. Fold in the dill. Season with a generous pinch of nutmeg and black pepper, and mix well. *(CONTINUED)*

Fill a dish large enough to hold one sheet of matzo with lukewarm water. Quickly submerge a sheet of matzo in the water, allow any excess water to drip off, and place in the prepared baking dish. You can also hold the matzo under a running faucet for a few seconds. The goal is to quickly wet the matzo and make it less brittle—it should not stay in the water long enough to get mushy. Wet a second piece of matzo and lay it in the pan next to the first, overlapping slightly if necessary.

Top the matzo with the spinach and feta mixture and spread evenly over the matzo. Wet the last 2 pieces of matzo, and place side by side on top of the filling. Drizzle with the olive oil, cover the pan with foil, and bake in the preheated oven for 35 minutes. Remove the foil and continue baking for 5 to 10 minutes more, or until the matzo is golden.

Remove from the oven and allow to rest for 5 to 10 minutes before cutting into squares and serving.

STORAGE: *Leftover spanakopita will keep, covered or foil-wrapped, in the refrigerator for 1 to 2 days. Warm in a 300°F oven to heat through and crisp the matzo before serving.*

# Cauliflower "Couscous" with Vegetable Tagine

*Sometimes, looking outside the Passover recipe box sparks the best holiday recipe ideas. As gluten-free and Paleo diets started trending, chefs, food writers, and bloggers looked for creative ways to fill the grain void. Cauliflower "couscous" is one wildly popular result, and it's perfect for Passover. Here, it's topped with a vegetarian tagine that can be adapted to include whatever vegetables you've got on hand. Feel free to omit the cumin if you consider it kitniyot.*

*Prep time: 25 minutes*
*Cook time: 45 minutes*

## FOR THE TAGINE

2 tablespoons extra-virgin olive oil

1 small onion, chopped

4 large garlic cloves, chopped

1½ teaspoons cumin (optional)

1 teaspoon ground ginger

1 teaspoon cinnamon

1 large sweet potato, peeled and cut into 1-inch chunks

2 cups water or vegetable stock

2 carrots, peeled and sliced

1 medium zucchini, cut into 1-inch chunks

1 medium yellow squash, cut into 1-inch chunks

1 large red bell pepper, cored, seeded, and cut into 1-inch pieces

4 Roma tomatoes, seeded and cut in eighths, or 1 (15-ounce) can diced tomatoes

Sea salt

Freshly ground black pepper

## FOR THE CAULIFLOWER "COUSCOUS"

1 large head cauliflower, cored and broken into florets

2 tablespoons extra-virgin olive oil

2 large garlic cloves, peeled and smashed

## FOR THE GARNISH

Harissa or hot sauce

Slivered almonds

Golden raisins

Finely chopped parsley

**MAKE THE TAGINE:** In a large chef's pan or Dutch oven set over medium-high heat, warm the olive oil. Add the onion and sauté until soft and translucent, about 5 to 7 minutes. Add the garlic, cumin (if using), ginger, and cinnamon. Sauté until fragrant, about 1 minute. Stir in the sweet potato, tossing to coat with the spices.

Pour in the water or vegetable stock. Add the carrots, zucchini, yellow squash, red pepper, and tomatoes.

Bring to a boil, reduce the heat to low, and partially cover the pan. Simmer, stirring occasionally, until the vegetables are tender, about 25 minutes. Season with salt and pepper, remove from the heat, and let rest while you make the cauliflower.

**MAKE THE CAULIFLOWER "COUSCOUS":** Place the cauliflower in the work bowl of a food processor fitted with an S blade. Pulse several times until the cauliflower is very finely chopped and resembles couscous. (If you don't have a food processor, simply use a box grater to coarsely grate the florets.)

In a chef's pan or large, deep skillet, warm the olive oil. Add the garlic and sauté for 30 seconds. Working in batches if necessary, add the cauliflower and sauté until crisp-tender and warmed through, about 3 to 5 minutes. Transfer to a serving bowl.

To serve, spoon the "couscous" into shallow bowls. Top with the vegetable tagine. Pass the harissa or hot sauce, slivered almonds, raisins, and parsley for garnish. Or, for a family style presentation, spread the "couscous" in a large, rimmed serving platter. Make a well in the center, spoon in the vegetable tagine, and sprinkle with almonds, raisins, and parsley. Offer harissa or hot sauce on the side.

**STORAGE:** *The cauliflower and tagine will keep, covered, in the refrigerator for 2 to 3 days.*

Tip

Harissa is a hot chile-based condiment that hails from Tunisia and is popular across North Africa and in Israel. Recipes typically include garlic, olive oil, and sometimes spices such as cumin or coriander, and range from mildly spicy to absolutely fiery. You can find it in Middle Eastern or kosher markets, specialty grocers, or online.

Maple-Glazed Vegan
Challah (page 233)

# CHAPTER TEN

# Desserts and Bread

Maybe it's the way aroma triggers memory, but it's hard to think of bubbes without thinking of warm, cinnamon-laced or fruit-laden baked goods. There was always a tin of home-made cookies or mandel bread in my grandmother's kitchen. If we were running errands, she was sure to swing by the bakery, where the counter lady (no doubt a bubbe herself) could be counted on to slip me a cookie. Or maybe the connection between sweet treats and grandmothers is so strong because these are the recipes they were most likely to make with us as children, helping us mix and roll dough, cut out cookies, or lick spoons. I still remember making hamantaschen with my grandmother, and now my kids do the same with theirs. I'm sure those associations are what make the treats so delicious.

# Dried Plums and Apricots with Almond Paste and Almonds

MAKES 40 TO 50 | PAREVE

*There may be no simpler confection than these naturally sweet treats. Every Purim, my grandmother stuffed crunchy almonds into sticky sweet prunes, as they were called then. She'd also sandwich marshmallows between apricots. My mom and I have taken up the tradition, though I like to give both fruits the almond treatment. I add almond paste to my version, both because it looks pretty, and because I love the multidimensional almond flavor and texture it contributes.*

*Prep time: 20 minutes*

1 (7-ounce) tube almond paste
20 to 25 plump pitted dried plums (prunes)
20 to 25 dried apricots
25 to 45 whole raw almonds

### Tip

You can use either sweet Turkish apricots or the more tart California apricots. Either way, look for plump fruit, which is both tastier and easier to stuff. Make sure to buy almond paste, and not marzipan, which is too sweet to complement the fruit well.

With clean, dry hands, pinch small pieces of almond paste from the log and roll gently between your palms to form hazelnut-size balls. Place the almond paste balls into the indentations in each prune. Top the almond paste in each prune with an almond, and press gently to secure.

Repeat the process with the apricots, but flatten the almond paste balls slightly before placing them between the apricot halves, like a little sandwich. Add an almond if you'd like. (Feel free to skip them if you don't want to surprise anyone with the unexpected crunch of a hard nut inside the soft fruit!)

**STORAGE:** *Store in an airtight container in a cool, dry place for 3 to 5 days, or in the refrigerator for up to 2 weeks. If refrigerated, bring to room temperature before serving.*

# Chocolate Oat Bars

MAKES 20 TO 24 | DAIRY OR PAREVE

*Long before gluten-free and paleo diet adherents embraced almond flour, my grand-mother and Bubbe, like countless kosher cooks, used ground nuts in their Passover baking. Armed with a sense of the perks and limitations of working with nut meals, thanks to those holiday recipes, I've taken to experimenting with them year-round. These bars were a happy accident. I planned to try my hand at a healthier version of blondies, but couldn't resist adding some oats . . . and then cocoa powder . . . and before I knew it, I had an entirely different recipe on my hands. If a brownie and crunchy oat granola bar fell in love and had babies, they'd probably look (and taste!) something like this. The bars may crumble at the edges a bit when you cut them; save the crumbs for stirring into yogurt or topping ice cream.*

*Prep time: 15 minutes*
*Bake time: 25 to 30 minutes*

1 cup white whole-wheat flour

1 cup almond flour (or almond meal)

1 cup old-fashioned rolled oats

⅓ cup sugar

¼ cup cocoa powder

¼ teaspoon sea salt or kosher salt

¾ cup neutral oil, such as canola or grapeseed

¼ cup unsalted butter, or virgin coconut oil, melted

2 large eggs

1½ teaspoons pure vanilla extract

1 cup dark chocolate chunks or chips

### Tip

If you use coconut oil, you may see it bubbling up around the bars when you pull them from the oven. If they're firm to the touch and seem otherwise well baked, don't worry— the oil will absorb back into them as they cool.

Preheat the oven to 350°F. Grease a 9-by-13-by-2-inch pan.

In a large bowl, whisk together the flour, almond flour, oats, sugar, cocoa powder, and salt. Stir in the oil and melted butter or coconut oil. Add the eggs and vanilla and mix well to combine. Stir in the chocolate chunks.

Transfer the batter to the prepared pan and spread with a spatula to the edges, pressing down gently to close any cracks. Bake in the preheated oven for 25 to 30 minutes, or until set. Cool in the pan on a wire rack before cutting into squares or rectangles with a sharp knife.

STORAGE: *These bars will keep, covered, for up to a week at room temperature. Or wrap them in foil and store in a freezer-safe container in the freezer for up to 3 months.*

# Whole-Grain Sunken Peach and Raspberry Cake

SERVES 6 TO 8 | PAREVE OR DAIRY

*"Can also use peaches." It's just a little notation on her Jewish Apple Cake recipe card, penciled in cursive, contained in parentheses. But it's proof that my grandmother wasn't afraid to tinker with a classic recipe and take it in new, delicious directions. That little scrawl in her hand inspired this Sunken Peach and Raspberry Cake, a more casual take on her holiday showpiece. This recipe is enriched with whole-grain flour, and skips the layering, so it's simpler to prepare. And because fresh or frozen peaches and raspberries both work, it's a nice recipe to pull out in the depths of winter, when you start to crave a little summer sunshine. If using frozen fruits, just make sure to thaw them first.*

*Prep time: 20 minutes*
*Bake time: 50 to 60 minutes*

FOR THE FRUIT

2 peaches, peeled, pitted, and sliced
½ cup fresh raspberries
1½ tablespoons sugar
1 teaspoon ground ginger

FOR THE CAKE

1 cup white whole-wheat flour
½ cup all-purpose flour
1 cup sugar
1½ teaspoons baking powder
¼ teaspoon kosher salt or sea salt
½ cup neutral oil, such as canola or grapeseed
3 tablespoons orange juice or milk
2 large eggs
1½ teaspoons pure vanilla extract

STORAGE: *The cake will keep at room temperature, covered in foil, for up to a day. (Cool completely before covering.) For longer storage, refrigerate, covered, for 2 to 3 days.*

Preheat the oven to 350°F. Grease a 9-by-9-by-2-inch baking pan.

In a medium bowl, mix all the fruit. Sprinkle evenly with sugar and ginger and toss to coat.

In a large bowl, whisk together the flours, sugar, baking powder, and salt. Add the oil, juice or milk, eggs, and vanilla, and mix with a whisk or electric beater just until smooth. The batter will be thick.

Pour the batter into the prepared pan, smoothing the top. Take the peach slices from the bowl and arrange over the batter, then sprinkle evenly with the raspberries.

Bake in the preheated oven for 50 to 60 minutes, or until the cake is set, the top is golden brown, and a cake tester inserted near the center comes out clean. Keep in mind that areas of cake right beneath the fruit will have a moister texture and crumb.

Cool the cake on a wire rack in its pan. Serve warm or at room temperature.

# Savta's Semi-Famous Jewish Apple Cake

SERVES 10 TO 12 | PAREVE

*If there's a dish that epitomizes the recipes once shared via carefully handwritten index card, this is it. What sets my grandmother's apple cake apart is that she used lots of apples, cut very thin, and meticulously layered them throughout the cake. It's not as simple as spreading chopped apples between two layers of batter, but it's a much better way to suffuse the cake with apple-cinnamon goodness. What made this cake semi-famous? Long ago, my sister walked into Bibi's, her favorite kosher bakery in Los Angeles, to find the owner poring over a recipe printout. It turns out it was an earlier version of the very one you see here. The owner laughed at my sister when she claimed the recipe was her grandmother's—until she pointed out my byline. I ended up offering him some advice on adjusting the recipe for a commercial bakery; his version is now a Rosh Hashanah bestseller.*

*Prep time: 25 minutes*
*Bake time: 1½ to 2 hours*

6 small apples (see tip), peeled, cored, and thinly sliced

3 tablespoons sugar

1 tablespoon cinnamon

3 cups all-purpose flour, plus extra for dusting

2½ cups sugar

1 tablespoon baking powder

½ teaspoon salt

1 cup expeller-pressed canola, grapeseed, or walnut oil, plus extra for greasing

4 large eggs

⅓ cup orange juice

1 tablespoon pure vanilla extract

Preheat the oven to 350°F. (If you are using a dark or nonstick pan, preheat to 325°F to prevent burning). Grease and lightly flour a large tube pan with a removable bottom. Tap out any excess flour and set aside.

In a large bowl, combine the sliced apples, sugar, and cinnamon. Gently toss to coat and set aside.

In another large bowl, whisk together the flour, sugar, baking powder, and salt. Using an electric mixer or a large wooden spoon, beat in the oil, eggs, orange juice, and vanilla, mixing just until the batter is smooth and thick.

Spoon about ⅓ of the batter into the prepared tube pan, then spread with a spatula to cover the bottom of the pan. With clean hands, arrange about ⅓ of the apple slices in an even layer over the batter, taking care to keep the apples from touching the walls of the pan. (This prevents sticking and makes it easier to unmold the cake.)

Spoon and spread a little less than half of the remaining batter over the apples. Don't worry if the batter doesn't quite cover the fruit, or moves some of the apples around. Top with about half of the remaining apples, reserving the most attractive slices for the final layer. Spoon the remaining batter over the second layer of apples, spreading with the spatula to cover them evenly.

Decorate the top of the cake with the reserved apple slices, arranging them in slightly over-lapping concentric circles—they will spread out during baking. If there's any syrupy cinnamon-sugar liquid left in the apple bowl, drizzle a little of it over the cake.

Place the cake pan on a rimmed baking sheet or on top of a piece of foil to catch drips. Bake on the center rack of the preheated oven for 1½ to 2 hours, or until a cake tester comes out clean

and the top of the cake is golden and crusty in spots. Test at the 1½ hour mark. If the cake isn't ready, test at 15-minute intervals until the tester comes out clean.

Remove the cake from the oven and allow it to cool in its pan on a wire rack. When it's completely cool, run an offset spatula or knife around the edge of the pan, then remove the outside of the cake pan. Next, run the spatula or knife between the underside of the cake and the pan bottom to loosen.

Over a plate, carefully invert the cake and slide it off of the tube and pan bottom. Place a serving plate face down on the cake. Hold both plates and flip, so the cake is now resting apple-side up on the serving plate.

STORAGE: *The cake will keep at room temperature, wrapped well in foil, for 2 to 3 days. Leftovers may also be frozen, double wrapped in foil and sealed in a freezer bag, for 1 to 2 months.*

Tip

Sweet-tart multipurpose apple varieties make the best apple cake. I like to use a mix of varieties, like Gala, Fuji, Lady Alice, Cameo, or Granny Smith.

# Russian Tea Cakes

MAKES ABOUT 40 COOKIES | DAIRY

*This recipe was a mainstay of my childhood, though it doesn't come from my grandmother, as I'd originally assumed. My mother started making the cookies we knew as "Meltaways" with her Hadassah group, and they subsequently showed up at countless family parties and potlucks. The original recipe used ground walnuts, but Ema decided she preferred hazelnuts, so she switched. Somewhere along the line, Nana Elsie's cookies (page 219) supplanted them as her go-to recipe. But thinking back on how much I loved helping roll the warm cookies in powdered sugar, I decided to put them back in the rotation with my own kids. And since the dough is eggless, I can even let them lick the mixing spoon.*

*Prep time: 30 minutes*
*Bake time: 15 minutes*

FOR THE COOKIES

¾ cup (1½ sticks) unsalted butter, cut into small pieces, at room temperature
2 cups all-purpose flour, sifted
½ cup confectioners' sugar, sifted
1 cup ground hazelnuts or walnuts
½ teaspoon salt
1½ teaspoons vanilla extract

FOR THE SUGAR COATING

2 cups confectioners' sugar

Preheat the oven to 350°F. Line two baking sheets with silicone baking mats or parchment paper. (Ungreased baking sheets are fine too).

Place the butter in a large bowl, or the work bowl of a stand mixer. Using an electric beater or the mixer's whisk attachment, cream the butter on low speed until smooth and fluffy.

Add the flour, confectioners' sugar, ground nuts, salt, and vanilla. Beat at medium speed until the dough is well mixed and has a sandy texture.

With clean hands, scoop up about a tablespoon of dough and gently roll it into a walnut-size ball. Place on the cookie sheet. Repeat with the remaining dough, spacing the baking about an inch apart on the baking sheets.

Bake in the preheated oven for 12 to 15 minutes, until the cookies are firm and very lightly browned.

Leave the cookies on their baking sheets and transfer to racks to cool slightly. Place the remaining confectioners' sugar in a medium bowl. Line a counter with parchment or wax paper and place another cooling rack atop it.

When the cookies have cooled enough to handle, drop them a few at a time into the confectioners' sugar. Roll them in the sugar until coated, then transfer to the cooling rack set over the parchment-lined surface, allowing space between the cookies.

**STORAGE:** *Once they are completely cooled, place the cookies in an airtight container with parchment or wax paper between each layer. Store at room temperature for up to 2 weeks. Or freeze, well-wrapped in foil and placed in an airtight container or freezer bag, for up to 2 months.*

Simple Swap

To vary the look and flavor of the cookies, divide the confectioner's sugar used for coating them between 2 or 3 small bowls. Roll some of the cookies in plain confectioner's sugar, and add cinnamon and/or cocoa powder to the other bowl(s) before coating the remaining cookies.

IN THE KITCHEN WITH
# LIZ REUVEN

*My first food memories swirl around scents of baked onions and toasted cinnamon. They emanated from separate bundles but wafted into our home simultaneously, nestled into freshly baked rolls and flavoring simple, child-friendly cookies.*

*My grandfather Simcha was a trained baker from a poor village in Galicia (now Poland). He and my grandmother Bertha were step-brother and sister, although they only lived under the same roof for a short time before arriving in America. Here, Gramps' specialty was "Jewish breads." He baked sweet, bronzed challot, dense rye breads flecked with caraway seeds, and my favorite: onion rolls.*

*Nanny was an ingenious home baker who was inspired to experiment out of necessity. She baked egg-free and dairy-free cookies for my sister Jill and our cousin Dayle. They were bonded by their shared allergies to dairy, eggs, chocolate, and nuts. Nanny figured out her own recipes so she could bake for "the girls," never wanting them to feel deprived of sweets.*

*There weren't any vegan cookbooks during the 1960s and '70s, but even if there had been, she couldn't have read them. In addition to being a fiercely determined home baker, she was illiterate. This quiet fact made her recipe development all the more astounding. Not only was she incapable of consulting other resources, but once she mastered her own recipes she never wrote them down, relying on her memory to duplicate the successes and avoid the failures.*

*Nanny's cinnamon-flecked kichel were moist, golden, and forever imprinted on my memory. She exercised her creativity by shaping these simple cookies into small mounds, twisted ropes, and lighthearted wriggles. She baked with oil and apple juice, as the girls were both allergic to orange juice, and a bit of baking powder instead of eggs. She spooned strawberry and apricot jams, long simmered on her stove, into her thumbprint in the dented rounds. In the autumn, she moistened the dough with homemade apple and pear purées made from fruit we picked together during Sunday outings in "the country."*

*Each Sunday, Nanny and Gramps arrived at our home with their paper bundles and unconditional hugs. Gramps brought golden, square rolls, with moist onions nestled in sweet dough. Nanny carried her own peckl with pride. Nanny's goodies were meticulously wrapped in wax paper and then again in brown paper to ensure that they stayed fresh between her pre-Shabbat baking and Sunday lunch with "the girls."*

*Today, I'm in awe of Nanny's determination. She was a vegan baker before her time, developing doughs and cookies with ingenuity and love rather than eggs and butter.*

LIZ REUVEN is the founder and editor of *Kosher Like Me*, a food blog and resource for those seeking vegetarian, organic, and other kosher-friendly foods.

# Pumpkin Halvah Bars

MAKES 16 TO 20 BARS | DAIRY

*My grandparents would occasionally pick up a block of halvah, a sesame-based confection, from the local kosher deli. I loved its unusual crumbly-melty texture, and the way its flavor flirted with savoriness. That my mother didn't like halvah somehow made it all the more intriguing. I shared a taste for it with Saba and my father; it was their special treat, and only I got to share nibbles of it. I'd never baked with halvah until I created these bars, and was looking for an accent to the sweet, spiced cake. Sesame, it turns out, makes a wonderful complement to pumpkin, and the little bits of halvah practically melt into the bars, while maintaining their own special character.*

*Prep time: 20 minutes*
*Bake time: 35 to 40 minutes*

1 cup all-purpose flour

½ cup packed brown sugar

¼ cup sugar

1 teaspoon cinnamon

1 teaspoon ground ginger

¾ teaspoon baking powder

¼ teaspoon sea salt or kosher salt

1 cup plain pumpkin purée, homemade
   or canned

6 tablespoons melted butter, cooled
   to room temperature

2 large eggs

1½ teaspoons pure vanilla extract

2 ounces vanilla halvah, chopped
   (about ¼ cup)

Preheat the oven to 350°F. Grease and flour a 9-inch baking pan.

In a large bowl, whisk together the flour, sugars, cinnamon, ginger, baking powder, and salt.

Add the pumpkin, butter, eggs, and vanilla, and whisk just until evenly combined and smooth. Fold in the halvah.

Pour the batter into the prepared pan. Bake in the preheated oven for 35 to 40 minutes or until a tester inserted in the center comes out clean. Cool on a wire rack before cutting into squares.

# Nana Elsie's Czechoslovakian Cookies

MAKES 4 DOZEN COOKIES | DAIRY

*Most of my grandparents' relatives lived in Philadelphia, and I relished the trips we made to visit the extended family. I especially loved visiting my Aunt Annette and Uncle Rob. I only had a couple of young cousins at home, but they had four "big" kids I idolized (plus an adorable dachshund), and were great entertainers too. We'd sometimes trek across the backyard to the neighboring house, where Annette's sister's family lived. Nana Elsie, the family matriarch, lived there too. This recipe is hers, and has held a place of honor in my family's cookie repertoire for years.*

*Prep time: 20 minutes*
*Bake time: 1 hour*

2 cups (4 sticks) unsalted butter, cut into chunks, at room temperature

2 cups sugar

4 large egg yolks

4 cups all-purpose flour

2 cups ground walnuts or hazelnuts

1 cup preserves, jam, or marmalade

**STORAGE:** *Store in an airtight container with wax or parchment paper between each layer of cookies. They will keep at room temperature for 1 week. Or freeze them, well wrapped in foil and placed in an airtight container or freezer bag, for up to 3 months.*

Simple Swap

These cookies work nicely with a half-and-half mixture of all-purpose and white whole-wheat flour as well.

Preheat the oven to 325°F. Lightly grease a 13-by-9-by-2-inch pan.

In a large bowl using a stand mixer, electric hand mixer, or rotary beaters, cream the butter and sugar together until light and fluffy. Add the egg yolks and continue beating on low speed until the mixture is a pale lemon color. Add the flour and ground nuts, and continue beating until evenly mixed.

Spoon half the batter into the prepared pan. With a spatula or clean hands, spread the batter to cover the bottom of the pan evenly.

Spread the jam, preserves, or marmalade over the batter, taking care to leave a ¼-inch border around the edge of the pan. Top evenly with the remaining batter, and smooth with a spatula so the jam is mostly covered.

Bake in the preheated oven for about 50 minutes to 1 hour, or until the top is golden.

Allow the cookies to cool on a rack in their pan for 30 minutes. With a sharp knife, cut into 1½-inch squares. Carefully remove the cookies from the pan with a spatula.

# Aunt Clara's Hazelnut Chocolate Chunk Cookies

MAKES ABOUT 3 DOZEN COOKIES | PAREVE

*Aunt Clara was one of my grandmother's dearest friends and though she wasn't actually related to us, she may as well have been. (To this day, my mom and aunt call her sons "brother"; her grandkids are our "cousins.") She'd have happily lived on Cheddar cheese and coffee, but she wanted to make sure everyone else ate well, and was an excellent cook and baker. Her Passover chocolate chunk cookies, flecked with ground hazelnuts and rich with hand-chopped chocolate, are so good that I actually prefer them to normal year-round cookies.*

*Prep time: 20 minutes*
*Chilling time: 1 hour, or overnight*
*Cook time: 12 minutes*

2 large eggs

¾ cup sugar

½ cup grapeseed or extra-virgin olive oil

1 cup Passover cake meal

2 tablespoons potato starch

½ cup ground hazelnuts (hazelnut flour)

3- to 4-ounces bittersweet or semisweet bar chocolate, chopped, or ½ cup pareve chocolate chips

In a large bowl, whisk together the eggs and sugar. Stir in the oil, cake meal, and potato starch, and mix until well combined.

Add the ground hazelnuts, and stir until they're thoroughly mixed into the dough. Fold in the chocolate, mixing until the pieces are evenly distributed. Cover the bowl and chill for at least 1 hour, or overnight.

Preheat the oven to 400°F. Line two baking sheets with parchment paper or aluminum foil. Using clean, oiled hands, take walnut-size chunks of the chilled dough and roll it into balls between your palms. Place the dough balls about 1½ inches apart on the prepared baking sheets. Flatten the balls with your palm or a spatula to about ¼-inch thick.

Bake the cookies in the preheated oven for 10 minutes, or until they begin to turn a light golden brown. Transfer the cookies to racks to cool.

**STORAGE:** *Once cool, store cookies in an airtight container at room temperature for 2 weeks, or well-wrapped in the freezer for up to 3 months.*

# Chocolate Orange Ricotta Cheesecake

SERVES 8 TO 10 | DAIRY

*My grandmother adored orangettes—a classic confection of candied orange peel dipped in dark chocolate. I wanted so much to like them, and would taste them whenever she offered. But the peel's residual bitter notes always put me off, and I'd ultimately opt for her other favorite, the arguably more kid-friendly cherry cordials. I eventually grew to share her love of orangettes, and their chocolate-orange flavor pairing was the inspiration for this ricotta-based cheesecake.*

*Prep time: 15 minutes*
*Bake time: 1 hour, 15 minutes*
*Chilling time: 6 hours, or overnight*

### FOR THE CRUST

1 cup finely crushed graham crackers (regular or chocolate)
2 tablespoons unsalted butter, melted

### FOR THE CHEESECAKE

15 ounces whole-milk ricotta cheese, drained
8 ounces mascarpone cheese
½ cup sugar
1½ teaspoons finely grated orange zest
⅓ cup cocoa powder
2 tablespoons all-purpose flour
3 eggs, lightly beaten
¼ cup heavy cream
2 tablespoons orange liqueur
½ cup finely chopped dark chocolate or mini chocolate chips

### FOR THE GARNISH

Plain or chocolate-covered candied orange peel (optional)

**MAKE THE CRUST:** Preheat the oven to 350°F. Lightly butter an 8- or 9-inch springform pan. In a small bowl, combine the graham cracker crumbs and melted butter, mixing well to coat. Press evenly into the bottom of the springform pan. Set aside.

**MAKE THE CHEESECAKE:** In a large bowl, whisk together the ricotta, mascarpone, sugar, and orange zest until evenly mixed and a creamy texture. Sprinkle the mixture evenly with the cocoa powder and flour. Whisk until smooth.

Add the eggs, cream, and orange liqueur. Whisk until all the ingredients are incorporated. Fold in the chopped chocolate or chocolate chips.

Pour the chocolate-cheese mixture into the crust in the springform pan, then gently smooth the surface with a spatula. Bake on the center rack of the preheated oven until the cake is set (a slight jiggle at the center is fine, but the cake should be mostly firm), about 1 hour to 1 hour, 15 minutes.

Remove from the oven. On a wire rack, cool the cake in its pan to room temperature, about 30 to 45 minutes. Run an offset spatula or sharp knife around the perimeter of the pan. Cover with tin foil, and place the cake, still in its pan, in the refrigerator. Chill for at least 6 hours, or overnight.

To serve the cake, unclip and lift off the pan's side. Leaving the cake on the springform base, transfer to a cake plate or serving platter. Garnish with plain or chocolate-covered orange peel, if desired.

# Poppy Seed Hamantaschen Dough with Fruit Filling

MAKES 4 TO 8 DOZEN, DEPENDING ON SIZE | DAIRY OR PAREVE

*Many years ago, when a cookie plate trend swept through the New York City restaurant scene, I was inspired to make mini hamantaschen. I mixed poppy seeds into the dough as a culinary wink to the poppy filling known as mohn, though my family's hamantaschen were always strictly a fruit-filled affair. I didn't know it at the time, but while going through my grandmother's recipes for this book, I discovered that her poppy cookies were remarkably similar to the dough I devised so many years ago. I don't recall ever eating those cookies, but I must have been channeling her when I dreamed up these hamantaschen.*

*Prep time: 45 minutes*
*Chilling time: 30 minutes*
*Bake time: 12 minutes*

4 ¼ cups all-purpose flour

1 ½ tablespoons poppy seeds

2 teaspoons baking powder

½ teaspoon salt

1 cup sugar

3 large eggs

¾ cup oil

⅓ cup orange juice

2 teaspoons pure vanilla extract

Lemon curd or preserves for filling

In a large bowl, whisk together the flour, poppy seeds, baking powder, and salt.

In another large bowl, whisk together the sugar and eggs until they're a light lemon yellow color. Add the oil, orange juice, and vanilla, and whisk well to mix.

Add the dry ingredients to the wet ingredients. Mix well with a wooden spoon or clean hands. Divide the dough in half, and shape into two discs. Wrap in plastic and chill in the refrigerator for 25 to 30 minutes.

Preheat the oven to 350°F. Line two baking sheets with silicone liners or parchment paper. Unwrap a disc of chilled dough and place on a lightly floured surface. Use a rolling pin to roll out the dough to about ⅛-inch thick.

Use a drinking glass or a 3- to 4-inch round cookie cutter to cut out rounds from the dough. For mini hamantaschen, choose a cup with a

2- to 2½-inch diameter rim, such as a sake cup or small juice glass. Transfer the rounds to the prepared baking sheet.

Spoon some lemon curd or preserves in the center of each round, taking care not to overfill. You'll need about 1 to 1½ teaspoons of filling for large rounds, or about ½ teaspoon for mini rounds.

Pull the edges of dough up around the filling, and pinch the ends to seal the edges together and form a triangle. The filling should be visible at the center.

Bake the hamantaschen in the preheated oven for 12 to 15 minutes, or until firm and golden. Use a spatula to transfer the hamantaschen from the baking sheets to a wire rack to cool. Repeat the process with the rest of the dough and filling.

STORAGE: *Once they are completely cooled, the hamantaschen can be stored in an airtight container with parchment or wax paper between the layers. Lemon curd–filled hamantaschen must be stored in the refrigerator. Preserve-filled hamantaschen will keep for 2 to 3 days at room temperature.*

# Tart Cherry and Dark Chocolate Granita Duo

SERVES 6 TO 8 | DAIRY OR PAREVE

*My grandmother's apartment complex had a swimming pool. She and her bathing-capped friends would do ballet stretches in the shallow end, then retire to an umbrella table to play Rummikub for hours while the grandkids splashed. The arrival of the snowball truck always meant a mass exodus from the pool. We'd line up for the frozen treats, and my grandmother—a great lover of cherry cordials—always got a cherry snowball with chocolate syrup. Sometimes, she'd charm the snowball man into sneaking a little vanilla ice cream into the mix. This pair of granitas is a grown-up take on that icy summer favorite. Best of all, you don't need an ice cream maker or ice crusher to craft the granitas—just a freezer, a fork, and a little patience!*

*Prep time: 10 minutes*
*Cook time: 10 minutes*
*Freezing time: 3 to 4 hours*

## FOR THE CHERRY GRANITA

2 cups unsweetened tart cherry juice

⅔ cup sugar

½ whole vanilla bean or ½ teaspoon pure
  vanilla extract

## FOR THE CHOCOLATE GRANITA

2 cups water

½ cup sugar

⅓ cup unsweetened cocoa powder

½ whole vanilla bean or ½ teaspoon pure
  vanilla extract

2 ounces dark or bittersweet chocolate
  chunks or chips

## FOR SERVING

Good quality vanilla ice cream or whipped
  cream (optional)

**MAKE THE CHERRY GRANITA:** In a medium, heavy-bottomed saucepan, combine the cherry juice and sugar. Scrape the seeds from the vanilla bean into the saucepan, if using, then drop in the pod. (If you are using vanilla extract instead, wait to add it until after the mixture has simmered.)

Over medium-high heat, bring the cherry juice mixture to a boil, whisking to dissolve the sugar. Reduce the heat to low and simmer, stirring occasionally, until the sugar is dissolved and the mixture reduces slightly, about 5 minutes. Remove from the heat. If you used a vanilla bean, remove the pod. If you are using vanilla extract, stir it in now.

Cool to room temperature. You can speed the cooling process by making an ice bath. Partially fill a large bowl with ice and cold water. Set another heat-proof bowl in the ice bath and carefully pour in the cherry mixture. Stir periodically until cool, about 5 minutes. *(CONTINUED)*

Pour the cooled cherry mixture into a
9-by-9-by-2-inch or larger pan. The granita
will freeze more rapidly in a metal and/or a
larger pan. Cover and place in the freezer for
45 minutes.

**MAKE THE CHOCOLATE GRANITA:** Rinse
the saucepan and add the water, sugar, and
cocoa powder. Whisk to incorporate the cocoa
powder, but don't worry if a few small lumps
remain. Scrape the seeds from the vanilla bean
into the saucepan, if using, then drop in the pod.
(If you are using vanilla extract instead, wait to
add it until after the mixture has simmered.)

Place over medium-high heat and continue
whisking to dissolve the sugar. Reduce the heat
to low and simmer, stirring occasionally, until
the sugar is dissolved and the mixture reduces
slightly, about 5 minutes. Remove from the
heat. If you used a vanilla bean, remove the pod.
If you are using vanilla extract instead, stir it in
now. Add the chocolate and whisk until it melts
into the mixture.

Cool to room temperature (use the ice bath
method). Pour the mixture into another
9-by-9-by-2-inch or larger pan. Cover and
place in the freezer for 30 to 40 minutes.

Remove the pans from the freezer. Use a fork
to break up the ice crystals that have formed
around the perimeter of the pans. Stir them
into the cherry and chocolate mixtures, respec-
tively, cover, and return the pans to the freezer.
Freeze for 30 minutes more, then stir the newly

formed ice crystals into the granitas, breaking
up any large ice chunks with the fork. Repeat
every 30 minutes until the mixtures are frozen
throughout and the texture has changed from a
slushy consistency to flaky crystals.

When both flavors of granita are totally frozen,
scrape again with a fork, then spoon some of
each flavor into serving dishes. Layer with a
little vanilla ice cream or whipped cream, if
desired. Serve immediately.

**STORAGE:** *The granitas are best served the day
they are made, but can be stored in an airtight
freezer container for up to 4 days. Thaw
slightly, and scrape to fluff the ice crystals
before serving.*

How-To

The chocolate and cherry granitas will
have slightly different textures and
freezing times, due to their different
ingredients. If the granitas freeze too
solidly to scrape and serve easily, leave
at room temperature for 5 to 10 minutes
to thaw a bit.

# Strawberry Trifle

SERVES 8 TO 10 | DAIRY

*Trifle was one of my grandmother's signature desserts, one that likely held sentimental associations for her, since her adored sister Rose was born in England. It's the recipe she chose to contribute to a 1976 luncheon hosted by her Hadassah group and the accompanying hand-bound recipe booklet, "Food Fancies from Foreign Lands." Though the title sounds quaint now, the recipes within—from Morocco, Denmark, Russia, Brazil, and more—were surprisingly authentic, and a testament to the diverse backgrounds of the women who shared them. The beauty of this dessert is that while it looks impressive and tastes divine, it's very easy to make, especially if you opt for store-bought cake and custard. Do follow my grandmother's advice to "Be generous with Cointreau."*

*Prep time: 20 minutes*

1 pint heavy cream

1 tablespoon sugar (optional)

1 (16-ounce) homemade or store-bought pound cake

Cointreau or Amaretto

2 cups vanilla custard or pudding

1 quart fresh strawberries, hulled and quartered or sliced

Raspberry or strawberry jam, warmed slightly for easy pouring

Place the cream and 1 tablespoon of sugar (if using) in a large bowl. Using an electric beater or a wire whisk, whip the cream until stiff peaks form. Set aside.

Cut the cake into ½-inch-by-2-inch "fingers." Place a layer of cake in the bottom of a trifle dish or a large glass bowl. Sprinkle generously with Cointreau. Spread with a layer of pudding, then a layer of whipped cream. Top evenly with a layer of strawberries. Drizzle with jam.

Continue layering with cake, Cointreau, pudding, whipped cream, berries and jam until the bowl is full. Use any remaining whipped cream or berries to garnish the top of the trifle.

Cover and chill cake until ready to serve. (My grandmother liked to make this a day ahead to let the flavors meld.)

**STORAGE:** *Leftover trifle will keep, covered, in the refrigerator 2 to 3 days.*

# Homemade Seeded Rye Bread

MAKES 1 LARGE LOAF | PAREVE

*Rye bread was a common fixture at my grandparents' house, whether for sandwiches, or my grandfather's garlic-rubbed rye toast. With such a great variety of bread flours on the market now, I decided to try my hand at a homemade rye bread, inspired by a recipe I found in my grandmother's collection. This one walks the line between a light and dark rye, and is as ideal for toasting as it is for sandwiches like the Roasted Beet Reuben (page 190) or Cloak and Dagger (page 180).*

*Prep time: 20 minutes*
*Rising time: 2 hours*
*Cook time: 35 minutes*

1 packet active dry yeast

1¼ cups warm water

2 cups all-purpose flour

1 cup white whole-wheat flour

1 cup rye flour

1½ teaspoons kosher salt or sea salt

2 tablespoons brown sugar

2 tablespoons molasses

2 tablespoons canola or grapeseed oil

1 tablespoon caraway seeds

In a large bowl, or the mixing bowl of a stand mixer fitted with a dough hook, combine the yeast and water. Let sit until foamy, 5 to 10 minutes. If the yeast doesn't react, discard the mixture and start again with fresh yeast.

In another large bowl, whisk together the flours and salt.

Add the brown sugar, molasses, oil, and caraway seeds to the yeast mixture. Add 2 cups of the flour mixture, and stir with a wooden spoon or mix on low speed for 1 to 2 minutes, until well blended. Then add the remaining flour.

Stir the dough well with a wooden spoon, then turn it out onto a lightly floured surface and knead for 5 to 10 minutes, until the dough is smooth, elastic and slightly tacky. Or mix it with the dough hook for 1 minute on low speed, then 3 to 5 minutes on medium speed, until the dough pulls into a ball and is smooth and slightly tacky but not sticky. Remove the dough hook. *(CONTINUED)*

Spread a little oil in the bowl (you don't need to clean it first), and place the dough ball back in the bowl. Cover with a tea towel or plastic wrap and set aside to rise until doubled in bulk, about 1 hour.

Punch down the dough, place on a lightly floured surface, and knead a few times. Shape the dough into a roundish oval, smoothing the top with your hands as you work. Place on a parchment-lined baking pan, cover, and set aside to rise 45 minutes to 1 hour.

Preheat the oven to 350°F. Use a sharp knife to make three or four shallow, diagonal slashes in the top of the loaf. Bake until the loaf is firm, golden on the bottom, and sounds hollow when tapped, about 30 to 35 minutes. Transfer to a rack to cool.

# Maple-Glazed Vegan Challah

MAKES 1 LARGE OR 2 MEDIUM CHALLAHS, OR 12 ROLLS | PAREVE

*Bubbe baked challah, but her recipe was lost. Savta baked a great deal from scratch, but when it came to challah, she went for convenience. She stuck to frozen, prebraided loaves that required only thawing and a rise before being baked in the oven. Or she'd pick up a challah at one of the neighborhood's many kosher bakeries. My mom always did the same. Perhaps because I had little frame of reference for doing it, baking challah from scratch seemed daunting. But I had friends who did it regularly, and after a few attempts of my own, I realized it's pretty straightforward, and a great intro to bread baking. My dad has even gotten in on the act, using his bread machine to experiment with dough recipes. While it takes a little planning timing-wise, the reward of homemade challah fresh from the oven is well worth the effort.*

*Prep time: 45 minutes*
*Rising time: 2 ½ to 3 hours*
*Cook time: 15 to 35 minutes*

### FOR THE CHALLAH

1¼ cups lukewarm water

6 tablespoons sugar

1 packet active dry yeast

¼ cup neutral oil, such as grapeseed or canola, plus extra for oiling the bowl

4 to 4½ cups all-purpose flour or 3 cups all-purpose flour mixed with 1 to 1½ cups white whole-wheat flour

2 teaspoons sea salt or kosher salt

### FOR THE GLAZE

1½ teaspoons pure maple syrup

1½ teaspoons soy milk or nut milk

**MAKE THE CHALLAH:** Place the water in a large bowl, or the mixing bowl of a stand mixer. Add a pinch sugar and sprinkle the yeast over the water. Set aside in a warm place for 5 to 10 minutes, until the mixture bubbles and turns foamy. If the yeast doesn't react, discard the mixture and start again with fresh yeast.

Add the sugar, oil, 2 cups of flour, and salt. With a hand whisk or the mixer's whisk attachment, mix until smooth. If using a stand mixer, swap the whisk attachment for the dough hook. Add the rest of the flour, 1 cup at a time, mixing after each addition with a sturdy wooden spoon or the dough hook until a shaggy dough forms and starts to pull into a ball. (Depending on the humidity and the flour's protein content, you may not need the last ½ cup or so. Only add it if the dough is very wet or sticky. Otherwise, save it to dust your work surface for kneading the dough.) *(CONTINUED)*

 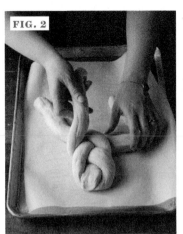 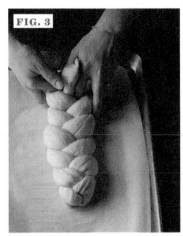

If you are using a mixer, allow it to knead the dough for 5 minutes, or until it is smooth and elastic. Otherwise, lightly flour a counter or table that's at a comfortable height for kneading. Turn the dough out onto the work surface and knead with clean, floured hands for 5 to 10 minutes, or until the dough is smooth and elastic and no longer has streaks of unincorporated flour.

Allow the dough to rest for a few minutes. If you used the mixer to knead, remove the dough from the hook and set aside. Clean and dry the large mixing bowl, and grease the inside with a little oil. Place the ball of challah dough into the bowl, and turn it to coat with the oil. Place a damp tea towel or plastic wrap over the bowl. Set aside in a warm place until the dough rises and doubles in bulk, about 1 hour, 45 minutes.

Lightly grease one or two baking sheets, or line with a silicone liner. Punch down the dough. Shape as desired.

For a traditional 3-strand braided challah, divide the dough into 3 or 6 equal pieces (depending on whether you are making 1 or 2 challot). Roll each ball of dough into a long, tapered strand. Lay 3 strands side by side (Fig. 1). Pinch the strands together at one end and tuck the ends under to secure. Starting with the strand on the right, braid the loaf by crossing first the right, then the left over the middle strand (Fig. 2). When you get to the bottom, pinch the ends together and tuck under the loaf (Fig. 3). Repeat the process if you are making a second loaf.

To make challah rolls, shape smaller pieces of dough into 12 strands. Take one strand and knot it in the middle, then tuck the ends under the knot. This makes one roll. Repeat with the remaining strands.

Transfer the shaped loaves and/or rolls on the prepared baking sheet(s). Cover with clean, dry tea towels. Let rise until doubled, about 45 minutes to 1 hour.

MAKE THE GLAZE: Preheat the oven to 350°F. In a small bowl, whisk together the maple syrup and soy milk. Brush the maple wash over the challah with a pastry brush (if you don't have one, a paper towel will do in a pinch). Bake until the challah crust is a deep golden brown and the loaf sounds hollow when tapped. A large challah will take about 30 to 35 minutes to bake. Allow 20 to 25 minutes for a medium challah, and 15 to 20 minutes for rolls. Transfer to wire racks to cool.

STORAGE: *The challah will keep, wrapped in foil, for 2 to 3 days at room temperature. Or place the foil-wrapped challah in a freezer bag and freeze for up to 3 months.*

How-To

To make the challah using a bread machine, the way my dad does, place the ingredients in the bread machine following the order recommended by your machine's manufacturer. Select the dough cycle. When the cycle ends, remove the dough from the machine. Proceed with the recipe starting with the first rise.

# PASSOVER

Passover has always been one of my favorite holidays, perhaps because it's the one I associate most closely with my grandmother. She'd extend the table from dining room to living room, hosting convivial Seders with as many guests as the apartment would allow. There's no time I feel her presence more than when we sit down to the Seders around my parents' extended table, in front of the same flower-strewn china my grandmother used, with delicate crystal her own mother carried over from Europe.

We enjoy her menu, now expanded with additions like quinoa and roasted asparagus. But my love of Pesach isn't so much about nostalgia, but of celebrating spring, freedom, and new beginnings. To that end, I focus on fresh produce, healthy cooking, and embracing the challenge of cooking almost entirely from scratch without familiar ingredients like flour. I fix my eye on what we *can* eat, instead of trying to duplicate what's off limits for the week, and find I enjoy the fresh perspective.

My aim in this section is to help with your Passover pantry stocking and menu planning for duration of the holiday. You'll find a chart of Passover ingredient substitutions, which is followed by an index of recipes in this book that are kosher for Passover, or may be adapted easily (with my notes for how).

# PASSOVER INGREDIENT SUBSTITUTIONS

| INSTEAD OF | SUBSTITUTE THIS |
|---|---|
| **1 cup all-purpose flour** | ⅝ cup matzo cake meal or ½ cup cake meal plus ¼ to ⅓ cup potato starch or 1 cup ground nuts or a combination |
| **bread crumbs** | Matzo meal or kosher for Passover panko |
| **1 cup buttermilk** | 1 tablespoon lemon juice, plus enough milk to make 1 cup—let sit 5 minutes before using |
| **1 cup confectioner's sugar** | 1 cup less 1 tablespoon granulated sugar, plus 1 tablespoon potato starch, pulverized in blender |
| **1 cup cornstarch** | ⅞ cup potato starch |
| **1 cup corn syrup** | 1¼ cups sugar plus ¼ cup water, simmered until syrupy |
| **Graham cracker crumbs** | Crushed Passover cookies, ground nuts, or a combination |
| **Margarine** | Virgin coconut oil (for nonbaking recipes, olive oil also usually works) |

| INSTEAD OF | SUBSTITUTE THIS |
|---|---|
| **1 cup matzo meal** | 3 broken matzos or 2 cups matzo farfel, finely ground in a food processor |
| **1 cup matzo cake meal** | 1 cup plus 2 tablespoons matzo meal, pulverized in a blender or food processor |
| **1 cup matzo farfel** | 1½ matzo sheets, crumbled into small pieces |
| **Peanut butter** | Kosher for Passover almond or cashew butter |
| **Schmaltz (chicken fat)** | 2 caramelized onions puréed until smooth, or olive oil |
| **1 ounce unsweetened baking chocolate** | 3 tablespoons cocoa powder plus 1 tablespoon butter, margarine, or oil |
| **1 cup vanilla sugar** | 1 cup sugar plus 1 split vanilla bean, sealed in an airtight container for at least 24 hours |
| **Flavoring extracts** | Lemon, orange, or lime juice or zest; brandy; amaretto; vanilla bean |

# INDEX OF PASSOVER RECIPES

It's easy to overlook when you're focused on the extra kosher restrictions on Passover, but lots of year-round recipes are perfect for the holiday as is, or with minimal adjustment. Here's a list of the recipes from this book that work for Passover, along with ingredient substitutes for those that need tweaking for the holiday.

Note that for Sephardim and those who eat kitniyot, the options are even more varied. For those unfamiliar with the term, kitniyot encompasses foods including rice, legumes, peas, corn, soybeans, peanuts, and certain seeds and spices including sesame, poppy, mustard, fennel, coriander, caraway, fenugreek, and anise. Whereas most Ashkenazim do not eat kitniyot during Passover, Jews of Sephardi and Mizrahi descent typically do eat some or all of them.

An asterisk denotes recipes that are non-gebrokts (matzo-free, and incidentally, gluten-free).

# YOM TOV (HOLIDAY) MENUS

From apples, honey, and pomegranates on Rosh Hashana, to matzo, wine, and charoset for Passover, every Jewish holiday has its own special food traditions. Drawing on the recipes in this book and accompaniments you can get at just about any grocery store, I've created special Yom Tov and Shabbat menus. Some are traditional, some are very new-school, but all incorporate holiday customs that have been passed down for generations.

## ROSH HASHANAH

Apples dipped in honey may be one of the most recognizable icons of Rosh Hashanah, the Jewish New Year, but they're far from the only symbolic holiday foods. Beets, pomegranates, carrots, winter squash, garlic, even fish heads—elegantly represented here as a whole, salt-crusted branzino—are traditionally eaten to ensure a sweet, safe, meritorious new year.

*Symbolic Menu for a Sweet New Year*

| | |
|---|---|
| | Wine, round raisin challah, apples, honey, and new fruits |
| 87 | Roasted Beet Salad with Ginger and Garlic Vinaigrette |
| 156 | Salt-Crusted Branzino with Herbs |
| 162 | Pomegranate-Lacquered Roast Chicken |
| 178 | Cranberry Horseradish Brisket |
| 110 | Orzo Salad with Roasted Carrots and Lentils |
| 95 | Butternut Purée with Roasted Garlic and Ginger |
| 212 | Savta's Semi-Famous Jewish Apple Cake |

# YOM KIPPUR

Yom Kippur, the Day of Atonement, is perhaps best known as one of Judaism's two 25-hour fast days. For all healthy adults over bar or bat mitzvah age, fasting is meant to help sharpen the focus on the spiritual work of the day. Going into the fast well hydrated and nourished is key to a (relatively) comfortable fast. After an intense day of reflection and prayer, joining with friends and family for a festive break fast meal is one of the joys of the Jewish calendar.

## *A Humble, Healthful Pre-Fast Meal (Seudat Ha'Mafseket)*

## *New School Break Fast*

# SUKKOT

The week-long harvest holiday of Sukkot falls fast on the heels of Rosh Hashanah and Yom Kippur, and culminates in the distinct but related holidays of Shemini Atzeret and Simchat Torah. In the Western Hemisphere, Sukkot tends to coincide with early fall, and (hopefully) weather nice enough for outdoor dining in the sukkot, or huts, meant to symbolize both the Israelites' dwellings as they wandered in the desert and the agricultural huts the nascent Jewish people used at harvest time once settled in ancient Israel.

## *Dinner Under the Stars*

## *Harvest Lunch*

# CHANUKAH

Chanukah, the midwinter festival of lights, celebrates the Maccabean triumph over the Greeks and the rededication of the holy temple in Jerusalem. It's an ideal time for a party, and if you're going to stand around flipping latkes, there's no need to complicate the rest of the menu. Since olive oil factors big in the Chanukah story, it's featured throughout the menu. There's a lesser-known tradition to eat cheese on Chanukah as a nod to the valiant Judith, who seduced and slew the Syrian-Greek general Holofernes with the aid of cheese, turning the tide of battle.

## *Latke Cocktail Party*

Beer, wine, cocktails

139   Butternut and Roasted Corn Chowder with Garam Masala

69    Za'atar Pita Chips

62    Muhammara

72    Feta and Olives with Oregano

59    Smoky Spice-Roasted Chickpeas

98    Potato Latkes with Ras el Hanout and Lemon Zest

Bakery sufganiyot (jelly donuts) and/or ice cream drizzled with olive oil

# PURIM

One of the mitzvot of Purim is to have a seudah—a festive meal. In tribute to Esther's heroism and the Purim story's Persian setting, this menu takes loose inspiration from Persian cuisine. Hamantaschen are a decidedly Ashkenazic dessert, but they're a Purim icon.

## *A Persian-Inspired Purim Feast*

Wine

169   Persian Chicken Stew with Tomatoes and Green Beans

102   Basmati Rice with Sweet Carrot and Orange

224   Poppy Seed Hamantaschen Dough with Fruit Filling

208   Dried Plums and Apricots with Almond Paste and Almonds

# PASSOVER

Passover celebrates the Exodus from Egypt and the liberation of the Israelite slaves into a free people. It's also a harvest holiday, dubbed Chag HaAviv (the holiday of spring), so the menus below—which will take you from the Seder through the week—focus on the fresh bounty of beautiful spring produce.

## *An "Old Meets New" Seder Menu*

77    Charoset Three Ways (sample of all three)

Matzo ball soup (using the recipe for Parsley and Nutmeg Matzo Balls, page 131)

166   Easy Apricot Chicken

177   Classic Brisket with New Potatoes and Carrots

112   Quinoa with Arugula, Butternut Squash, and Citrus Vinaigrette

93    Asparagus with Smoky Pepper Vinaigrette

227   Tart Cherry and Dark Chocolate Granita Duo

221   Aunt Clara's Hazelnut Chocolate Chunk Cookies

## LAG B'OMER

Counting the Omer—the 49-day period between Passover and Shavuot—ticks off the days between the barley offering and wheat harvests in ancient Israel. There's tension inherent in the count, both because of the long-forgotten realities of potential crop failure, and the better known mourning period associated with a plague (or possible military casualties) among Rabbi Akiva's students. Lag B'Omer—the 33rd day of the count—marks the end of the plague and the associated mourning. It's celebrated, especially in Israel, with barbecues and picnics.

## SHAVUOT

Shavuot is the third major harvest holiday of the Jewish calendar, and marks the giving of the Torah and the Israelites' official evolution into Jewish peoplehood. As a nod to their preparation to accept the Torah and the laws of kashrut, dairy foods are traditionally eaten. Stuffed foods, especially cylindrical ones that can be arranged like Torah scrolls on the plate, are customary too.

# TU B'AV

Tu B'Av—the 15th of Av—is little known today, but according the Talmud, it was the most important festival of the year. Following close after the mournful Tisha B'Av fast, Tu B'Av celebrates love and renewal. On Tu B'Av in ancient Israel, Jewish maidens would dance in the starlit vineyards, and suitors would come, hoping to woo their match. In Israel today, it has become a day of romance, and is now a popular day for engagements and weddings.

## A Romantic Tu B'Av Menu

|     | Prosecco or Cava |
| --- | --- |
|     | Prosecco or Cava |
| 126 | Watermelon Gazpacho |
| 154 | Black Bass with Burst Cherry Tomatoes and Herbs |
| 192 | Vegetarian Paella |
| 229 | Strawberry Trifle |

# SHABBAT

Every Friday, as dusk settles, Jews around the world usher in Shabbat, the Jewish day of rest. Meals are, ideally, convivial and unhurried, full of delicious fare that there's less time to enjoy during the hurry of the work week. These menus highlight the flow of the seasons. Since cooking is prohibited on Shabbat, the lunch menus feature make-ahead and no-cook recipes.

## Fabulous Fall Shabbat Dinner

|     | Wine |
| --- | --- |
| 233 | Maple-Glazed Vegan Challah |
| 164 | Marmalade-Roasted Chicken with Potatoes |
| 115 | Farro Salad with Lemony White Beans, Roasted Red Peppers, and Cauliflower |
| 96  | Maple Dijon–Glazed Brussels Sprouts |
| 47  | Apricot Pistachio Babka |

## Simple Springtime Shabbat Dinner

| 134 | Ruby Chard and Lemongrass Schav with Herbed Sour Cream |
| --- | --- |
| 153 | Moroccan-Spiced Cod with Oranges and Olives |
| 97  | Colcannon with Kale |
|     | Steamed or roasted broccoli |
| 214 | Russian Tea Cake Cookies |
|     | Clementines, tea |

## Summer Salad Shabbat Lunch

| 64  | Thai-Style Summer Rolls with Peanut Sauce |
| --- | --- |
| 151 | Orange Dijon Salmon (serve chilled) |
| 117 | Buckwheat Soba Salad |
| 105 | Forbidden Rice Salad with Mango and Ginger Vinaigrette |
|     | Green tea ice pops or mochi |

## Warming Winter Shabbat Lunch

| 88  | Grapefruit, Avocado, and Sardine Salad with Za'atar Croutons |
| --- | --- |
| 200 | White Bean Cassoulet |
| 218 | Pumpkin Halvah Bars |

# THE CLEAN FIFTEEN AND THE DIRTY DOZEN

**A NONPROFIT** and environmental watchdog organization called Environmental Working Group (EWG) looks at data supplied by the US Department of Agriculture (USDA) and the Food and Drug Administration (FDA) about pesticide residues. Each year it compiles a list of the best and worst pesticide loads found in commercial crops. You can use these lists to decide which fruits and vegetables to buy organic to minimize your exposure to pesticides and which produce is considered safe enough to buy conventionally. This does not mean they are pesticide-free, though, so wash these fruits and vegetables thoroughly.

These lists change every year, so make sure you look up the most recent one before you fill your shopping cart. You'll find the most recent lists as well as a guide to pesticides in produce at EWG.org/FoodNews.

## Clean Fifteen

| | |
|---|---|
| Asparagus | Kiwi |
| Avocados | Mangos |
| Cabbage | Onions |
| Cantaloupe | Papayas |
| Cauliflower | Pineapples |
| Eggplant | Sweet corn |
| Grapefruit | Sweet peas (frozen) |
| Honeydew melon | |

## Dirty Dozen

| | |
|---|---|
| Apples | Peaches |
| Celery | Snap peas (imported) |
| Cherries | Spinach |
| Cucumbers | Strawberries |
| Grapes | Sweet bell peppers |
| Nectarines | Tomatoes |

*In addition to the Dirty Dozen, the EWG added two types of produce contaminated with highly toxic organo-phosphate insecticides:*

Kale/collard greens

Hot peppers

# MEASUREMENT CONVERSION CHARTS

## Volume Equivalents (Liquid)

| US STANDARD | US STANDARD (OUNCES) | METRIC (APPROXIMATE) |
| --- | --- | --- |
| 2 tablespoons | 1 fl. oz. | 30 mL |
| ¼ cup | 2 fl. oz. | 60 mL |
| ½ cup | 4 fl. oz. | 120 mL |
| 1 cup | 8 fl. oz. | 240 mL |
| 1½ cups | 12 fl. oz. | 355 mL |
| 2 cups or 1 pint | 16 fl. oz. | 475 mL |
| 4 cups or 1 quart | 32 fl. oz. | 1 L |
| 1 gallon | 128 fl. oz. | 4 L |

## Oven Temperatures

| FAHRENHEIT (F) | CELSIUS (C) (APPROXIMATE) |
| --- | --- |
| 250°F | 120°C |
| 300°F | 150°C |
| 325°F | 165°C |
| 350°F | 180°C |
| 375°F | 190°C |
| 400°F | 200°C |
| 425°F | 220°C |
| 450°F | 230°C |

## Volume Equivalents (Dry)

| US STANDARD | METRIC (APPROXIMATE) |
| --- | --- |
| ⅛ teaspoon | 0.5 mL |
| ¼ teaspoon | 1 mL |
| ½ teaspoon | 2 mL |
| ¾ teaspoon | 4 mL |
| 1 teaspoon | 5 mL |
| 1 tablespoon | 15 mL |
| ¼ cup | 59 mL |
| ⅓ cup | 79 mL |
| ½ cup | 118 mL |
| ⅔ cup | 156 mL |
| ¾ cup | 177 mL |
| 1 cup | 235 mL |
| 2 cups or 1 pint | 475 mL |
| 3 cups | 700 mL |
| 4 cups or 1 quart | 1 L |

## Weight Equivalents

| US STANDARD | METRIC (APPROXIMATE) |
| --- | --- |
| ½ ounce | 15 g |
| 1 ounce | 30 g |
| 2 ounces | 60 g |
| 4 ounces | 115 g |
| 8 ounces | 225 g |
| 12 ounces | 340 g |
| 16 ounces or 1 pound | 455 g |

# INDEX

# ACKNOWLEDGMENTS

TREMENDOUS THANKS to everyone who helped make this book possible. To editor and sounding board extraordinaire Stacy Wagner-Kinnear, for wondering if I might have some bubbe stories to tell, and for entrusting me with this project. To photographer Evi Abeler, food stylist Laurie Knoop, and their cadre of amazing volunteers for making the recipes come alive in such gorgeous fashion. I'm indebted (and eternally grateful) to Mitchell Davis, Ronnie Fein, Kim Kushner, Liz Reuven, Paula Shoyer, and Alexandra Zohn for sharing their own grandma stories, memories, and recipes. They've made the book incomparably richer with their contributions. To Beth Heidi Adelman and Robin Maltz for their sharp eyes, sharper queries, and enthusiastic help in shaping the manuscript. To Katy Brown for the beautiful design, Corinne Kalasky for getting the word out, and to everyone at Callisto who helped bring *Bubbe and Me* to fruition.

Special thanks to Ema, Aba, Shani, Doda Ita, and Aunt Merle for sharing their family memories, and the recipes that sparked them. And most especially, thank you to my sweet kids, Riva and Gabe, the best little kitchen helpers I could ask for, and to Dan for your love, support, kid-entertaining mojo, and eternal willingness to taste whatever recipes I dream up.

# ABOUT THE AUTHOR

**MIRI ROTKOVITZ** is a food writer, editor, recipe developer, and registered dietitian. She got her start in food writing at the James Beard Foundation, and has since turned her eye to food trends, nutrition questions raised by modern food processing, and the evolution of the kashrut industry. Inspired by Jewish tradition and culinary history, her passion lies in adapting recipes and experimenting with new techniques to create delicious, healthful, and creative kosher meals. As the kosher food expert for About.com, she shares recipes, entertaining tips, and articles exploring kosher culture online at kosherfood.about.com. She lives with her family near Baltimore.